Sabine Both

Love in my Luggage

Aus dem Deutschen
von Helena Ragg-Kirkby

Thienemann

The rival

"I'm so fed up," I said, annoyed, and proved my point by grunting into the telephone receiver like an angry **moose** during the **mating season**.

Jan **sighed** down the other end of the telephone wire. Poor thing. He really wasn't having an easy time of it with me at the moment. For days I'd been inflicting my murderous mood on everyone. And for days I'd been ringing Jan every five minutes to **moan** at him. Okay, best friends have to put up with that sort of thing, but Jan really did deserve a medal. The medal for super-human mega-patience.

"Lana, just look on the bright side ..." he breathed in a tone of voice that might perhaps be good for calming startled chickens. It hadn't worked for ages on me, though.

"The bright side?? How on earth am I supposed to see the bright side? I'm not even allowed to be there! Even before it's appeared, I'm **cast aside**! As of

---

moose – Elch
mating season – Paarungszeit, Brunftzeit
to sigh – seufzen; to moan – jammern, stöhnen
to cast sb aside – jmdn. links liegen lassen

today, I'm as unimportant in this family as needlework lessons are at school!"

Whilst I continued to wail into Jan's ear, I tried to get a view of the living room through the keyhole. However, I could only see a tiny portion, through which my father was rushing to and fro like a fleeing criminal. One time he was carrying a **scented candle**, then a pile of sofa cushions, then a bottle of **elderberry** juice. But whatever he carried past, it never seemed to be the right thing.

"What can you see?" Jan wanted to know.

"Not much. They've made everything all dim. My mother's lying on a heap of bedcovers like the Princess and the Pea. But all I can see are her feet. And this stupid **midwife** is **crouching** in front of them, staring. I hate that woman. She's in a good mood from morning till night. As if bringing babies into the world was the greatest thing in the universe. Being a midwife is the most stupid job there is. I'd rather be a dustman than become a midwife."

"And what are they saying?"

"I can't hear. They've got loud music playing. Just so that I don't hear anything. And you know what? I'd rather not hear anything anyway. I'd rather pack my suitcase and move into a **hostel**. Or somewhere. Doesn't matter where."

"My mum said that births like that aren't for children. Maybe it's not directed against you."

---

scented candle – Duftkerze
elderberry – Holunder; midwife – Hebamme
to crouch – hocken, kauern; hostel – Wohnheim

Did Jan really have to **blather on** so sensibly right now? Couldn't he just say: Lana, you're right. Your parents **are bananas**. You're being treated unjustly. Your life is a catastrophe. Did he always have to be so diplomatic?

Okay, so my parents had in fact had one of those "come and sit down on the sofa" conversations with me, and they'd explained that birth was a completely natural thing, but that it was too much for children. So I was supposed to go and stay with Mum's friend Carola when it got to that point. But since it wasn't supposed to get to that point until the day after tomorrow, Mum's friend Carola wasn't there when it all started. And as it all started much more quickly than they expected, Dad no longer had the nerve to find anyone else for me. And so he'd bundled me off to my room and had stuck headphones on me with *The Three ???* in the cassette player. I've not listened to *The Three ???* for two years. And never in a situation like this.

"And the fact that my mother took at least two minutes to remember my name the day before yesterday wasn't directed at me either. That's for my own good as well, presumably? 'La... La... La...'. My own mother forgets the last two letters of my name. Well, thanks a lot!"

"Lana, that's **bound to be** the hormones. Pregnant women have tonnes of hormones."

---

to blather on – endlos weiterquatschen
to be / go bananas – verrückt sein / werden
to be bound to be – etwas ganz bestimmt sein

"Hormones. Hormones. That's all I ever hear. My mother is full of them. And at school all the girls are cracking up, **cackling** at everything, and are in no state to have any kind of normal conversation. And all because of hormones. After all, I don't have hormones."

"You're bound to get some, too."

"I'm not letting any hormones into me, I can promise you that!"

"Okay. You'll be the only person to be spared hormones." Jan sighed again.

And my stomach started to rumble loudly. "What's more, I'm hungry. I could starve, and they wouldn't care. They'll soon have a replacement anyway."

Jan's sigh turned into a groan, almost as tortured a groan as my mother gave when it suddenly got to that stage.

"Be quiet, Jan, I think I can hear something."

In between the drumming rhythm of Mum's stupid **chakra** record I could hear quite strange noises now.

"Sounds like my great aunt's **St. Bernard** after running a hundred metres in the **scorching** heat."

My mother was **panting**. Not that I wasn't already familiar with this panting. After all, Mum had been panting for months in her **antenatal class**, and

---

to cackle – gackern
chakra – indische Musikart
St. Bernard – Bernhardiner
scorching – sengend; to pant – hecheln
antenatal class – Geburtsvorbereitungskurs

she'd been practising at any inappropriate moment: during meals, on the toilet, watching TV, and when she picked me up from school. But this panting had absolutely nothing to do with the gentle breathing in and out of the last few months. This panting made your blood run cold in your veins.

"What's happening?" asked Jan impatiently.

"I don't know. The midwife's looking pretty crazy and she's waving her arms around Mum . . . now she's got a really angry face, and she's shouting at Mum. Something about pushing . . . And now she's looking as if she's wet herself . . . and now . . . Oh my God!"

"Lana? Lana? Are you still there?"

"Jan. That's disgusting!"

"What? What's disgusting?"

If I'd have known what it was, I'd gladly have told Jan. But I wasn't sure. The midwife was holding something in her hands. Something revoltingly blueish. And before I could even decide if it was an alien or not, she'd taken it out of my line of vision. Now all I could see were Mum's feet, which were still moving round in circles. Mum's feet go round in circles when she unwraps Christmas presents, when she eats chocolate mousse, and when Dad massages her neck. Why on earth were they going round in circles when Mum was being presented with a disgusting blueish thing?

"Lana?"

"I reckon it's arrived," I said resignedly.

And at the same moment Dad came running into my room.

"Finn's arrived!"

Not without my best friend

Over the next few weeks baby madness spread across my family like an epidemic. Nobody but me could speak German any more; they all just babbled in goo-goo language. I was the only one who was immune to this swee-e-e-e-t virus. Everyone else went around **grinning like Cheshire cats**.

Amidst all this, Finn screamed from morning until evening. However, it didn't give my parents a nervous breakdown, but just made them even keener to look after him.

"Couldn't you just eat him up?" squealed Mum.

And Dad, Granny, Great-Granny and everyone who came and went to look at the baby agreed.

"You could eat him up!"

I was tempted to fetch salt and pepper from the kitchen, but an inner voice told me that it wasn't such a good idea. Where babies were concerned, eating things up was different from eating up waffles with **whipped cream**. Eating up meant something

---

to grin like a Cheshire cat – sehr breit und ausdauernd grinsen
whipped cream – Schlagsahne

like 'not knowing where to put all that love'. I knew very well where to put the love for my brother. It fitted easily under the bitten nail of my little finger.

I wanted nothing to do with **the whole palaver**. But that didn't seem to interest anyone. Nobody was interested in me at all any more. It made no difference if I got an A for Maths or had to confess that I'd had my name written in the register: my parents acknowledged everything with the same vacant smile.

The only function I still seemed to have was as an information service. The telephone rang the whole time. I felt as if I was working in a call centre. *How may I help you?*

"Has he got any hair?"

"How much does he weigh?"

"Does he look like you?"

He's as bald as Homer Simpson, probably weighs the same as a Christmas turkey, and doesn't look remotely like me! I'd have liked to have answered, but I surprised them with detailed facts.

"A bit of **down**, pale yellow, eight pounds, no, he looks like a distant uncle."

How was something so completely shrivelled supposed to look like me? I'd stood by his **crib** a couple of times and had looked at him more closely. Who knows, I thought, maybe I'd missed something. But despite all my efforts, I couldn't find the remotest thing interesting about him. It was dead boring in

---

the whole palaver – das ganze Theater
down – *hier:* Flaum
crib – Krippe, Wiege

his company. You couldn't tell him anything; he didn't understand jokes; he couldn't even sit up, **never mind** stand, never mind play basketball. He normally **dribbled** or cried. If I hadn't had Jan, I'd have gone mad.

"Let's do something that doesn't begin with B or F," I said firmly.

"B for Baby? F for Finn?" Jan asked **shrewdly**.

I nodded.

"Lana, are you sure? What about our favourite occupation? That begins with B, too."

Oops. I'd not thought about that. I quickly changed the rules. "Well, we are, after all, in Germany. Here, we don't call the little things babies; we call them infants. So, then, nothing that begins with I or F. Basketball's fine!"

After all, basketball with Jan was the best medicine for bad moods caused by Is and Fs.

"Surprise!" boomed Dad very first thing on a Sunday morning, raising my **blind** with a hideous push, and dragging me out of the realm of baby-free dreams into **dummy**-filled reality.

I couldn't bear it when people woke me up first thing in the morning with an overdose of good humour. And I could bear it even less when someone

---

never mind – geschweige denn
to dribble – sabbern
shrewd – scharfsinnig
blind – Jalousie
dummy – Schnuller

else went over my head and decided what time I should get up at the weekend. At the end of the day I wasn't a baby any more, and I was most probably able to decide for myself when and how much I wanted to sleep, eat and drink. But since Howler had been here, all our bio-rhythms evidently had to change.

"Lana, wake up! We've got some great news. Come on! Come on!"

To cap it all, Dad then started to grope under the bedcovers and made a grab for my feet. Whether I wanted it to or not, my blood pressure rose with anger **of its own accord**.

"I'm coming!"

With difficulty I struggled out of bed and **slunk** into the kitchen, where Mum was already waiting with Finn at her breast. She was in just the same horribly good mood as Dad.

"We decided last night that we're not going to stay at home for the holidays after all," declared Dad.

"We're going to rent a little house by the sea in Holland. That's okay for Finn, too. The fresh air will do him good," added Mum.

"Just the four of us. We'll really relax for once. Then you can do a bit more with your little brother. That's bound to improve your mood," Dad ended his lecture.

Two weeks in Holland with my mentally **be-**

---

of its own accord – eigenständig
to slink – verstohlen schleichen

fuddled parents and the little howler were supposed to lift my mood?

"So why am I never asked?"

Mum and Dad were completely **baffled**.

"Don't you want to go on holiday?" asked Dad, confused.

"Who's interested in what I want!"

"Lana, you know we always take your opinion into account."

Mum really didn't need to come along being all social-worker-teacher-like.

"Oh yeah? And did you ask me for my opinion about having him over there?" I pointed at Finn, who squealed loudly with **glee** as if to say: I don't care.

Mum and Dad were evidently lost for words. I felt that I was in the absolutely superior position. I was in the right. And that was something Mum couldn't discuss out of existence.

As the silence was just starting to become unbearable and I was wondering if I really was so completely in the right, Finn started to scream his head off. That was my opportunity to make a dramatic exit. Whilst Mum and Dad were bending over Finn, I grabbed my jacket and rushed off.

"I'm not going on holiday with them. What am I supposed to do there?" I asked Jan.

---

befuddled – durcheinander
baffled – verblüfft
glee – Heiterkeit

"We're not going away at all," said Jan, "because Dad wants a new car."

That was just like Jan's dad. Jan's parents and my parents couldn't possibly be more different. Whilst my parents **leapt** from one drumming course to the next, read one another's Tarot cards, **hummed mantras** to help me to sleep, and spent ages discussing who should take parental leave, Jan's dad always wore a suit and dreamed of a top-of-the-range Mercedes. Jan's mother had an embittered look around her mouth, and **stags**' heads hung on the walls of their living room.

But we were as similar as our parents were dissimilar. We were best friends. Soul mates. Blood brothers. And **beneficiaries**. Jan was the beneficiary of my Will, and I was of his.

"That's stupid." I gave Jan a gentle punch in the ribs.

"Yes. Now I have the choice between holidays at home or holidays with my grandparents. Thanks a bundle. You know my granny: *'No, Jan, don't sit on that cushion. It's only intended to be* ***ornamental****'.*"

I had experienced Jan's granny a couple of times in the flesh. She really was dreadful.

"No, Jan, don't sit on the ***loo*** *seat. It's only intended to be ornamental,"* Jan **trilled** on.

---

to leap – springen
to hum – summen; mantra – indische Gebetsformel
stag – Hirsch; beneficiary – Nutznießer, *hier:* Erbe
ornamental – zur Zierde
loo – Klo; to trill – trällern

I shook with laughter. *"No, Jan, don't eat the biscuits, they're only intended to be ornamental!"* I added. *"No, don't breathe the air, it's only intended to be ornamental!"*

We kept throwing phrases like this at each other, slid further off the bed onto the floor with every remark, and ended up doubled up with laughter.

Suddenly I had a gigantic flash of inspiration. "Come with us!"

Jan got it immediately. "Do you think it would be okay?"

"It has to be okay!" I was so excited by my idea that I didn't want to wait a single second longer to turn it into reality.

As if something had bitten us, we fled to Jan's mum in the living room and both babbled at the same time.

"Can I?"

"Can he?"

"Ple-e-e-e-e-ase!"

Jan's mum looked severely at us over the top of her glasses. She couldn't cope well with so much **commotion** because of her migraines. So we pulled ourselves together. It wouldn't do to annoy anyone now!

"You'll have to ask your father," she said to Jan.

That was how things were with Jan's parents. Somehow the father had more of an opinion than the mother. And he made all the important decisions.

---

commotion – Aufruhr

Jan didn't look very happy. "He's bound to say no."

Jan's father mostly said no on principle. You got the feeling that he hadn't even gathered exactly what it was all about before he **invariably** said no.

I thought. "Then I'll have to persuade my parents first. If they personally ask your father, he can't say no."

At home I didn't find the best preconditions for a big request. Mum and Dad were cross that I'd just run off. Just running off wasn't allowed in our house. After all, we could talk about everything.

"If you've got something on your mind, you can talk to us," Dad started immediately.

They just didn't understand that I couldn't talk and didn't want to talk when I was overcome with anger.

"We're very sorry if you're not getting your fair share at the moment," said Mum in a **conciliatory** tone.

That was my chance. If Mum felt bad, I should take advantage of it.

"You could easily make up for it right away," I said, **as sweet as pie**.

"Go on?" asked Dad suspiciously.

"Yes, I've just got one little wish. Can Jan come on holiday with us?"

---

invariable – unweigerlich
conciliatory – versöhnlich
as sweet as pie – zuckersüß

Mum and Dad exchanged a lengthy look. It seemed to me as if hours would pass. Was there some kind of telepathic connection between them? Whatever the case, they somehow seemed to have agreed about the matter because Dad finally nodded.

"Okay."

I immediately ran to **hug** him, and then Mum, too. "You're the best!"

If they weren't the worst parents in the entire galaxy at the moment for bringing a howler into the world, they really were the best.

"And there's just one more little thing. Jan's father ..."

Jan's father was the victim of Mum's unbeatable arguments and her trusting manner. He agreed.

I was happy.

---

to hug sb – jmdn. fest an sich drücken

Dud hits the back of someone's head

"Wow!"

We jumped out of the totally overloaded car and excitedly ran around our holiday home. It was fantastic. An old farmer's cottage with an overgrown garden, right behind the sand dunes.

Inside everything was really cosy and **comfortably appointed**. There was a long dining table, an open fire which was probably more use in winter, two bedrooms and a brand-new sauna in amongst all the antique stuff.

Jan and I **bagged** the room with the nicest view.

"I'm having the bed by the window!"

"No, I want that one!" I **screeched**, running at Jan with full force. He fell onto the bed and tried to **get me in a headlock**.

But I wasn't going to make it that easy for him. We

---

dud – Blindgänger
comfortably appointed – mit allem Komfort
to bag sth – etwas für sich reservieren
to screech – kreischen
to get sb in a headlock – jmdn. in den Schwitzkasten nehmen

had a **top-notch** wrestling match, which nobody won because we were both completely out of breath after ten minutes.

"A draw. Let's just push the beds together. Then we'll both be next to the window," I said.

"**Deal**."

We let go of one another and I stayed lying on Jan's stomach, as floppy as a **flounder**. Only then did I see that Mum was standing in the doorway, scrutinizing us critically.

"What's the matter?" I asked. "You'd presumably have discussed it fully, wouldn't you? But we do things differently!"

Jan and I laughed. Mum didn't.

"Oh, nothing," she said, lost in thought, and went out of the room.

"What's the matter with her?" Jan asked.

"No idea. But I'll find out," I answered, and **crept** off after Mum.

She sat herself down on the bed in her bedroom and watched Dad sorting out the linen. I **peeped** cautiously round the door.

"I need to talk to you." Mum's voice sounded as if she had a genuine problem.

Dad sat down next to her. "What's the matter?"

"Do you think it's a good idea for Lana and Jan to sleep in the same bedroom?"

---

top-notch – erstklassig
deal – Abmachung, Handelsgeschäft
flounder – Flunder; to creep – kriechen
to peep – verstohlen gucken

"Why?"

That was exactly what I was asking myself, too. What on earth could be not a good idea about it?

"She's 13. And Jan's already 14." Mum looked anxiously at Dad.

"You think ... no!" replied Dad. "I just can't imagine it. They're mates. I mean ... they're like brother and sister ... I mean, you know. Lana is herself more like a boy."

"Yes, you're probably right. All the same. I'm not entirely comfortable with the situation. Our daughter isn't a child any more."

Incredible. So far as I could see, my parents were just talking about whether Jan and me sharing a room could be a **saucy** situation.

What nonsense! We'd already slept in the same bed a thousand times.

I'd heard enough, and ran back to Jan to give him a report.

"You won't believe it. They think we might **get off with** one another."

In order to emphasise the absurdity of the whole thing, I put my arm round Jan's throat and bit him on the neck **under the pretence** of passion.

"Take me!" I breathed as **huskily** as I could manage.

I'd expected that Jan would completely enter into

---

saucy – pikant, frech
to get off with sb – mit jmdm. Sex haben
under the pretence – dem Anschein nach
husky – lüstern-heiser

my little theatrical interlude, but nothing happened. During my short absence the humour control centre in Jan's brain had somehow become blocked.

With an angry movement he pulled my arm off his shoulder and pushed me away. "Very funny."

"Yes, I found it funny at any rate. What's wrong with you? You're acting as if you had hormones now as well," I **teased** him.

Aha. Now the blockage seemed to have cleared. Jan grinned.

He slapped himself on the cheek. "That was a hormone! Got it just in time." Then he started on me. "Oh, Lana, hormones everywhere!"

After we'd successfully **fended off** all the hormones and were lying on the bed, completely exhausted, it occurred to me that I'd almost forgotten the most important thing.

"I have to say hello to the sea!"

"Eh?"

"It's like my start-of-holiday ritual. It's really important! I go to the sea and say hello. Doesn't matter if it's the Mediterranean, the Baltic, the Atlantic or the North Sea. And without wanting to **offend** any of the seas, I have to say that the North Sea is my most favourite of all. See you later then!"

I raced up the dunes and when I'd got to the topmost point, I took a deep breath of the sea air into

---

to tease sb – jmdn. necken
to fend sth off – etwas abwehren; to offend – beleidigen

my lungs. Then I **nosedived** down to the beach with outstretched arms and closed eyes. Oh, was that lovely …

"Ow!"

Did that ever hurt! I'd **slap, bang, walloped** into an obstacle. And when I opened my eyes, dazed, I found myself face to face with a boy who, like me, had fallen backwards during our crash and had landed on his bottom.

"Can't you watch what you're doing?" he snapped. He rubbed his nose. I had obviously hit him hard.

"I'm sorry. I didn't see you."

"Hardly surprising. I wouldn't see anything with my eyes shut either." He recovered himself, stood up, turned round, and brushed the sand off his clothes.

He was a head taller than me and was burnt brown by the sun. His black hair was cut mega-short. No wonder. The back of his head was really **gorgeous**.

"The back of your head is really gorgeous," I heard someone saying.

And that someone was me. Why on earth had I said that?

The boy looked at me, **repelled**. "And you've got **a screw loose**."

He turned and stamped off, shaking the back of

---

to nosedive – im Sturzflug rasen
to slap, bang, wallop – volle Pulle mit etwas kollidieren
gorgeous – herrlich, prächtig; repelled – *hier:* angewidert
sb has a screw loose – bei jmdm. ist eine Schraube locker

his head as he went. I was left sitting in the sand, in no position to get up. As if paralysed, I stared after the back of his head. Whatever was wrong with me? Had I got **concussion**? Or did I in fact really have a screw loose?

When I got back home, everything was already unpacked, and Dad was cooking spaghetti. Jan had hung my clothes up in the wardrobe, put my toothbrush in the **mug** and was in a great mood.

"What's happened to you?" Jan cautiously touched my forehead with his **index finger**.

"Ouch."

"That really is a big bump," he stated in a **consultant-like** manner.

"Don't I just know it!"

"How did that happen? Did the sea beat you up when you said hello to it?"

This time my humour control centre was blocked. "Very funny. I ..." I hesitated. I didn't want to tell him about the back-of-the-head. I quickly had to invent some story. "I collided with a **seagull**."

Jan looked at me with disbelief. "With a seagull?"

"Yes!" I jumped onto the bed. "I was running down the dunes minding my own business and all of a sudden ..." I stretched my arms out and **soared**

---

concussion – Gehirnerschütterung
mug – Becher; index finger – Zeigefinger
consultant-like – arztmäßig
seagull – Möwe
to soar – steil nach oben fliegen

like a monster gull over the mattress, "… this abnormally large seagull came right at me and banged into my forehead with its hard **beak**." I let myself fall off the bed. "I was totally knocked out. You've never seen anything like it."

Jan was impressed by my dramatic account. "I've never heard of gulls attacking humans."

"It was definitely a killer gull."

Over supper everyone talked about the killer gull. And after I'd told my absurd story brilliantly well for the third time, I almost believed it myself. I'd almost forgotten the embarrassing collision with the back-of-the-head boy.

What does it matter? I thought. I'll never see the back-of-the-head boy again. He can think what he likes about me. I'd probably had something like a mini concussion. That made people talk nonsense.

I was already fast asleep when Finn's squawking woke me up again. And I was so annoyed that I couldn't think of going back to sleep.

For a while I imagined a scenario in which a killer gull nosedived onto the beach at great speed, grabbed Finn by the **nappy** like a stork, and flew off with him for ever. It would leave him somewhere in the South Seas, and then he'd have a lovely life in the middle of the coconuts and coral reefs.

When the story stopped amusing me so much, I stared at the ceiling and tried to count sheep. One. Two. Three.

---

beak – Schnabel
nappy – Windel

What kind of sheep was that? It was much too big – and it walked on two legs. And it had a gorgeous back of the head. And instead of jumping over a fence, it boldly stood before my inner eye and tapped its forehead at me.

Curses! Hadn't I decided to forget what had happened? I banged my fist on the bedcovers with pure rage. Or, rather, I wanted to bang my fist on the bedcovers. Instead, I hit Jan. Thank God he didn't wake up. He turned over restlessly onto his other side and mumbled something. I strained my ears to hear.

"All **tosspots**," he mumbled.

I had to hold onto myself to stop myself from laughing out loud. That was too funny. He was presumably just dreaming about a basketball game and was cursing the opposing team. I carried on listening. But there was nothing more to hear except some **indistinct** mumbling.

I turned over onto my side and shut my eyes. Now I'd be able to sleep. And just as I'd almost managed it, yet another word reached me.

"Lana," Jan sighed in his sleep.

I'd obviously just scored a brilliant goal in his dream.

Curses! – Verdammt!
tosspot – Blödmann
indistinct – undeutlich

Howler

The next morning we packed all our beach gear and went to the sea. Dad painstakingly built a multi-dimensional windbreak.

"The little one mustn't get cold."

Mum coated herself in suncream and lay down in the sun. "I've earned this."

And Jan and I slipped into our swimming things and **plunged** into the waves. It was fabulous. We dived like seals, let ourselves be carried away by the current, and raced one another. Blue with cold and with red eyes from the salt water, we came back to the windbreak and wrapped ourselves in our towels.

For lunch there was a gigantic portion of chips from the beach kiosk, and then Mum and Dad wanted to have a walk along the sea to help their **digestion**.

"Half an hour of just the two of us for once. We'll leave Finn with you. He's just been fed, and he should sleep now. See you later."

"Fine," said Jan.

---

to plunge – (sich) stürzen
digestion – Verdauung

The words stuck in my throat. Nothing was fine! I thought. I don't want to be alone with the howler. But before I could say anything, Mum and Dad had already disappeared hand in hand.

I tried to relax, grabbed a newspaper and flicked through it. But it was as if some magnetic force were coming from the sleeping creature in his bed of blankets and towels, and I couldn't concentrate. I kept staring at Finn. Had he moved? Had I heard something? Irritating or what.

"I'm going back into the water." Jan jumped up and grabbed the **lilo**.

"You can't leave me alone with the baby!" I **pleaded** spontaneously.

Jan shook his head understandingly. "Everything else okay though, Lana?"

I nodded quickly and grinned. "Just wanted to see if you'd be **taken in**," I said quickly.

Of course, he was right. I was behaving in a **ludicrous** manner. What was nice about spending a few minutes alone with a baby behind the windbreak? Nothing was remotely nice about it.

"I wouldn't be taken in so easily by you!" cried Jan, and ran off towards the sea.

I tried again to concentrate on the article about snowboarders in Switzerland. But I must have read the first sentence five times without understanding what it meant.

---

lilo – Luftmatratze
to plead – flehen; to take sb in – jmdn. reinlegen
ludicrous – lachhaft, lächerlich

And then it happened. Without any warning, Finn began to scream his head off. Curses! What was I supposed to do now? I crawled over to him and looked into his worked-up red face. He looked as if he'd burst any minute.

"Shh," I said, and put my finger to my lips.

That had no effect.

"Be quiet!" I tried the non-gentle method.

He just howled even more.

"Goo-goo," I said.

That always worked for Mum and Dad. But it didn't work for me.

"So what do you want?" I eventually asked helplessly. "Would you be kind enough to tell me what I'm supposed to do?"

Funny **worm-like blood-vessels** were starting to show on Finn's forehead. He was now as bright red as an over-ripe tomato. Could babies explode?

Panicked, I looked towards the sea, but Jan was playing with the lilo right out at sea, and wasn't aware of my catastrophe.

"If you'll be quiet, I'll give you my sticker collection," I **stammered**. "Be quiet, and I'll give you my in-line skates, too."

Curses. Finn was **incorruptible** and tireless. His howling echoed in my head like a tornado. And suddenly **I blew a fuse**.

"Help!" I cried at the top of my voice. "Help!!!"

---

worm-like blood-vessel – wurmartige Ader
to stammer – stottern; incorruptible – unbestechlich
I blew a fuse – bei mir knallte eine Sicherung durch

Before I knew where I was, a woman came running up to me. In **next to no time** she surveyed the situation, picked Finn up, and rocked him to and fro in her arms. He went quiet immediately. I crouched on the ground like a poor sinner and struggled to hold back the tears.

The woman smiled at me. "He just needed a bit of attention," she said in a friendly manner. "You take him." She was about to **thrust** Finn into my arms.

I immediately turned away. "No. No. I'm allergic to babies. And anyway – he's not my brother. He's ... he's ..."

The woman looked at me, amused. "Simon was the same age as you when we had another baby. Believe me, it's difficult to start with. But at some point you'll realize how much you love your little brother."

Hadn't she listened to me? I'd just said that it wasn't my brother. And what did she know? Whoever Simon was, he had nothing in common with me. I would definitely never love the howler.

The woman laid Finn back in his bed. He fell asleep straight away and I said a quick prayer that he wouldn't wake up again until my parents got back.

"Simon!" called the woman.

The back of someone's head peeped out from behind the next windbreak. Oh my God. That wasn't **any old** back of the head. I knew the back of that head.

---

next to no time – null Komma nichts; to thrust – schieben
any old – ein x-beliebige(r/s)

"Come on over here."

Simon came closer, recognised me, and the smile immediately vanished from his face.

"This is ..." the woman introduced me, and waited for me to finish the sentence.

"Lana," I mumbled.

"And this is Simon. You can have a chat about little **siblings**." She waved to me and then left me standing alone with Simon.

His nose was somehow redder than the rest of his face. I touched my bump and grinned. Colleagues in combat!

Simon didn't grin. "I don't think that chatting is such a good idea," he said, and turned away.

"No, nor do I," I said quickly and quite casually, and turned away as well.

Something turned over in my stomach, crept up to my throat, and pressed like mad. I fled under the windbreak and hid my face deep in the hand towel. Whatever I did, I mustn't start crying loudly now! There wasn't even any reason to start crying. A strange boy who happened to have a particularly well-formed back of the head thought it wasn't a good idea to talk to me about little siblings. So what? After all, I didn't want to talk about Finn. And anyway, nobody has to like everybody they meet. There were enough people whom I couldn't stand. And I couldn't stand this Simon either. Not in the slightest. So he could hate me, too. That was only fair.

---

sibling – Geschwister

I **spat** vigorously three times in the sand and breathed deeply. Why didn't it work? All the other times I'd spat three times, I'd always had the feeling that I'd spat out everything I didn't want to have in my head any more. But this time everything stayed there.

How did Mum always do it? "My left arm is ve-e-e-ry heavy. I feel relaxed, and I am thinking of nothing." I'd always resisted joining in this stupid self-help training. But at that moment any method would do if it would make me get a grip on myself again.

I lay down flat on my towel and tried to explain to my arm that it had to go heavy. But it didn't do it. Instead, it just became more and more nervous, and I did, too. Invisible sand-flies **tugged** like mad at my body.

"Earth to Lana. Wow, you're easily scared today."

"I thought it was hormones," I said.

"How about that? You're the only person on earth who's immune to them," laughed Jan, flopping down on his towel.

I decided not to tell him anything about Finn's screaming **fit** and its consequences. I wouldn't tell Mum and Dad either. Otherwise I'd have to explain how I knew Simon and I'd have to admit that the killer gull actually had a lovely back-of-the-head. That was all much too complicated.

---

to spit – spucken
to tug – ziepen
fit – Anfall

A silly masquerade

The next day I didn't want to go with everyone to the beach.

"I'd just like to enjoy the garden," I said as casually as possible.

The fact was that I didn't want to meet Simon under any circumstances. When all was said and done, I found him abnormal. I didn't want to spoil my day by seeing him. Surely that was perfectly understandable?

"I'll stay here with you," decided Jan.

We sat on the terrace and played cards with one another. The sun burned down on our necks. As I'd already got a bit sunburnt yesterday, I wanted to use some suncream.

"You'll never reach," said Jan, taking the tube out of my hand. "I'll do it."

Jan took too much suncream and began to rub it into my back in **abundance**. It was really lovely. Jan must have noticed that I liked it, and carried on massaging me.

"Oh, yes. That's particularly nice," I sighed.

---

abundance – Überfluss

Jan had enormous **staying power**. He **kneaded** my neck. He kneaded my shoulders. He kneaded my arms.

"If nothing comes of playing basketball, you could become the masseur for the national team," I **burbled**. "Or you can be my private masseur when I'm named Player of the Year."

In my mind, I could already see myself being interviewed. *I already knew when I was eight years old that basketball was my life. Children? No, I never wanted children. I had a little brother, you know. After that experience, you know that babies are the plague. My masseur? Yes, he's my best friend. We've known one another for years.*

"Finished." Jan wiped his hands on his trousers. "Now you put cream on me."

I quickly slapped a bit of suncream on his back. "Finished. Let's carry on playing."

But I had got it all wrong. For whatever reason, Jan suddenly became bad-tempered and wanted to read. Fine by me! I thought.

Until three o'clock I managed to just think about nothing. Then Mum and Dad came back with Finn in their luggage.

"We met a really nice family. The Schneiders. A **teacher couple** with a twelve-year-old girl and a boy

---

staying power – Durchhaltevermögen
to knead – kneten, massieren
to burble – plappern
teacher couple – Lehrerehepaar

of Jan's age. They're coming to us for a barbecue this evening."

Please no! Dear God, don't let it be THE family. Make the boy of Jan's age have a really **dented** back of the head.

"The son is called Simon," said Mum as if she'd guessed my thoughts. "You've already met him, haven't you, Lana?"

Anyone with **perfect hearing** would definitely have heard the lump dropping down into my stomach like an earthquake.

For the rest of the afternoon I couldn't get my head together at all. I didn't want to read, I didn't feel like **chucking** things on the barbecue, I didn't want to do anything at all. I took myself off to my bedroom and **rummaged** around, unmotivated, in the cupboard.

There were so many people on the beach. Why did my parents have to come into contact with Simon's parents of all people? And why did my parents have to be so horrendously approachable? Why did they immediately have to start asking people to barbecues? Couldn't they be the kind of parents who didn't want anything to do with strangers? Like Jan's parents. They never invited anyone. And especially not **on the spur of the moment**.

---

to dent sth – etwas eindellen
perfect hearing – das absolute Gehör
to chuck – schmeißen; to rummage – wühlen
on the spur of the moment – ganz spontan

After I'd **churned up** my clothes cupboard, I began to check out Mum's clothes. Not that I was looking for anything. I just didn't know how else to kill the time.

I found the mini skirt that Mum never wore at home, and only wore on holiday for Dad's sake.

"It's much too tight for me. And anyway, I'm not twenty any more," she'd said.

I thought mini skirts were stupid. In fact, I found any kind of skirt stupid. They were much too impractical. I took Mum's mini skirt out of the cupboard and slipped into it. Silly. And much too big. Extremely silly.

My gaze fell on Mum's make-up bag. I thought make-up was stupid, too. I got a lipstick out and painted my lips. Silly. I looked as if I'd got a bang on the mouth rather than on the forehead. Extremely silly.

I pursed my lips. I thought kissing was stupid. Kissing was what you had to do to aunties when they gave you silly old soap for your birthday. When people kissed in films, I was always bored to death and was longing for the next action scene. Kissing was silly. I kissed the back of my hand. Just for fun, to see the shape of my lips. Extremely silly.

At that moment Mum came through the door. "Are you coming? What ...?"

I had hidden the lipstick behind my back, but that was of course ridiculous as my lips were blood-red.

Mum smiled. "Well, we're seeing a completely new side to you."

---

to churn up – durchwühlen

Oh please, not this **tack**. I hate it when I feel as if I've been caught **red-handed**. But what on earth have I been caught doing? I'd just tried on a bit of lipstick and put on a skirt. And I'd discovered, as always, that I found it completely silly. Was that anything to get worked up about?

"It really suits you," said Mum **conspiratorially**.

"No, it's silly," I replied **curtly**, and wiped the lipstick off.

Mum seemed to be thinking. Then she asked me, "So who did you want to make yourself so chic for?"

"I didn't want to make myself chic!"

Mum didn't seem satisfied with my answer.

"I wanted to shock Jan with how silly I looked," I added quickly.

"You wanted to look nice for Jan?"

"Shock him, not look nice for him!"

Wasn't she listening to me at all? But then I had a sudden realisation, and I remembered the conversation I'd overheard between Mum and Dad. Mum obviously felt that her worst fears had been confirmed. If her little girl was already putting on make-up and wearing a skirt for her boyfriend, then it wouldn't be long until the first kiss, and then ...

"Hey, Lana, you and Jan ..." Mum began cautiously.

"Mum," I quickly interrupted her. "I know what

---

tack – *hier:* Masche
red-handed – auf frischer Tat
conspiratorial – verschwörerisch
curt – kurz angebunden

you think. No, there's nothing going on. We're friends. And that's what we'll stay. And I'm not into all that whole girls-and-boys-kissing-cackling-sleepless-nights rubbish!"

Mum seemed relieved. "But if ..."

"Yes, Mum, if anything changes, I'll come to you and ask you for the Pill."

Mum's face fell like a landslide. She hadn't been prepared for anything like that. I laughed up my sleeve. It was so easy to shock her.

"Yes, fine," she said quickly and left me alone.

I **giggled** to myself. As if I'd ever take the Pill! There were all sorts of hormones in it!

I slipped out of the skirt and put my jeans on. Sometimes I didn't understand myself either. Hadn't I got anything better to do than dress up?

---

to giggle – kichern

These stupid hormones

I couldn't eat a single thing, but everyone else was having a great time. Dad and Herr Schneider were exchanging barbecue anecdotes. Mum and Frau Schneider were making a palaver about the horoscopes of their babies. Finn and Suse Schneider were lying together on a **fleece**, trying to outdo each other at kicking their legs around. And Simon Schneider and Jan had discovered within five minutes that they supported the same basketball team, and were listing all the players. Nobody was talking to me, though.

I pushed my sausage around my plate, **pronged** it with my fork, and imagined that it was Simon and that the tomato ketchup was a lake of blood. I found him more and more unbearable. What an ignorant imbecile.

"Lana plays fantastically well, too," said Jan.

He seemed to have noticed that I was sitting around like a little girl lost, and tried to bring me into the conversation.

---

fleece – Vlies, Schaffell; to prong sth – etwas aufspießen

"Oh," said Simon tonelessly, without taking any notice of me even for a second.

You arrogant **whippersnapper**, I thought. You repulsive, miserable **beanpole**! You ... you ... I was so angry that I was afraid that I might start howling at any moment. The blood pounded in my swollen forehead.

Mum laughed in my direction. "Lana should have been a boy. She's a textbook **Aries**. Wild and **stubborn**. Aren't you, Lana?"

I felt my bump swell up considerably.

"She's never played with dolls. Always cars and balls. She's never remotely known what to do with pretty dresses. Her favourite thing was always splashing around in the dirt."

All of a sudden, a whole heap of **jumping jacks** exploded in my bump.

"You've got no idea who I am!" I grabbed my blood-soaked sausage, tore it open, and chucked both halves at my mother's head.

I couldn't think any more. My legs became independent of me and ran away. Indistinctly, I could just hear Finn starting to howl. Then there was just a rushing in my ears.

I ran to the beach, threw myself on the sand, and howled with all my might. What on earth was wrong with me? Why was I crying? I never cried. I

---

whippersnapper – Schnösel; beanpole – Bohnenstange
Aries – *Sternzeichen:* Widder; stubborn – stur, starrköpfig
jumping jack – Knallfrosch

had never been so strange as I was today either. I was fully capable of contradicting a stupid remark. And anyway, what had Mum said that was so bad? She was right. I did think that I was more like a boy. And I was wild and stubborn, too. And proud of it. I was more confused than I'd ever been in my entire life. My head was spinning and my heart was pounding like mad.

I was just about to jump up and run into the sea to pull myself together with a cold-water shock when I heard a voice.

"Sweetheart."

Mum.

"What's the matter?"

She'd brought my jacket with her. I was in fact terribly cold. The thought of the cold water made it even worse. My teeth were already chattering. Mum took me in her arms and rubbed my back. It felt good.

"I'm sorry," I **whimpered**.

"It was only ketchup," said Mum, pointing on her T-shirt to a big red mark which looked like a bullet-hole in a thriller.

We had to laugh.

"Did I offend you with what I said?" Mum asked.

I **shrugged**. But she'd hit the nail on the head because the tears started to roll again at twice the speed.

"Could it be that something about you is chang-

---

to whimper – winseln
to shrug (one's shoulders) – mit den Schultern zucken

ing at the moment? I mean, something about being a girl?"

She'd scored another goal. All of a sudden, I saw everything very clearly. Yes, something had changed. And how! It wasn't just that hair was growing in the most impossible places, nor that I had a panic every month that those stupid towel things would slip when I was playing basketball; things had changed inwardly, too. I just hadn't wanted to admit it to myself.

"Nothing's where it belongs any more," I sobbed, and found the sentence totally stupid as I said it. It sounded as if someone had tidied my room and had messed up my own system by doing so.

"Sweetheart, that's perfectly normal at your age. It's the hormones. You're becoming a woman," said Mum, stroking my head. "It's horribly confusing to start with, but in time you'll realize how exciting and lovely it is."

"I can't see anything lovely about it," I **wailed**. "And I didn't let these stupid hormones creep into me!"

Mum could hardly keep a straight face. And, of course, she was right. I knew that hormones were formed in the body. But I just couldn't understand why my own body had conspired against me.

I blew my nose. "Now they'll all think I've **gone** completely **nuts**," I said despairingly.

Mum smiled at me. "Let's say a bit **tense**."

---

to wail – jammern; to go nuts – verrückt werden
tense – angespannt

I had to laugh whether I wanted to or not.

"Is it this Simon?" asked Mum.

I looked at her, surprised.

"You like him, don't you?"

A heap of potato salad and cement churned away in my stomach. Oh my God. She was right.

"The back of his head," I said tonelessly. "It's really just the back of his head."

"I can understand that," Mum smiled to herself.

"I don't actually like him at all," I tried to dismiss the terrible truth with one last show of resistance.

"No?" Mum grinned.

I shook my head **limply**. Why carry on lying? Lana, I said to myself, face reality. You don't hate him; you think he's fantastic. Don't ask why: just accept it as a fact.

"If you admit it to yourself, it's nowhere near so bad," said Mum. "It was obvious that you'd fall in love sooner or later."

Oh yes? Was it obvious? Not to me! I'd never even have dreamt that something like that would ever happen to me.

Mum **ruffled** my hair. "Who knows. Perhaps soon you'll let your hair grow."

She knew she couldn't say this without being punished. Mum had always wanted me to grow my hair. And I'd always told her that I'd rather run

---

limp – kraftlos, schlaff
to ruffle – zerzausen

around with a shaven head than have her do my hair in **pigtails** and **looped-up plaits**.

I **flung** myself at her, and we rolled around in the sand like the seals. At some point I got the upper hand, **squatted** on my squealing mother and held her wrists pinned down to the ground.

"**Have mercy**!" she laughed.

"If you absolutely have to have a child with long hair, then you can forbid Finn to go to the hairdresser's for the rest of his life!" I said **mock-threateningly**.

Then I let Mum go. After our little fight I did at least have the hormones sufficiently under control to get a grip on myself again.

"Mum, don't tell anyone I'm in love, okay? It's embarrassing."

"Okay. It'll be just between us women."

"And especially not Jan! Otherwise he'll think I'm completely useless."

When we got back, the Schneiders had already gone. Dad and Jan were washing up.

Jan immediately came up to me. "Is everything okay?"

"Yes. Everything's fine. Probably just some kind of sunstroke."

---

pigtail – Zopf
looped-up plaits – geflochtener Haarkranz
to fling – werfen; to squat – hocken, kauern
Have mercy! – Erbarmen!
mock-threatening – gespielt drohend

"I thought you'd gone nuts because of your killer-gull experience," Jan grinned.

"Ha ha! Did the others say anything?"

"Nothing."

"Nothing?"

I simply couldn't believe it. The mad way I'd behaved: surely someone must have said something.

"Simon thought what you did was cool."

"Cool?" I noticed my heart taking on a life of its own. **Thump**. Thump. Thump. Had he really said he thought I was cool?

"He said you were a real Terminator."

Oh my God! Of all the comparisons in the world, that was the worst. Hello, may I introduce myself? Lana, the Terminator. She's actually a boy, likes getting dirty, and throws sausages around.

---

to thump – pochen, klopfen

Once upon a time there lived a basketball star

"Simon is asking if we'll go and play basketball with him."

At first I didn't know if I was still dreaming or if I was awake. I was probably somewhere between the two.

"Us?" I **growled**.

"Yes, us," said Jan. "You and me. Earth to Lana. Wake up. I'll wait downstairs. Hurry up. Simon's already gone on ahead."

Wake up. Hurry up. That all sounded pretty complicated. Simon was waiting? For God's sake! That was one shock too much first thing in the morning. My stomach immediately started to work. That's what it normally only did after breakfast. Did being in love ultimately have something to do with digestion? And didn't you even get a break from this being in love first thing in the morning on an empty stomach?

I dragged myself into the bathroom and stared into the mirror. God help me! I looked as swollen as a fat **toad**. Crying had devastating consequences for

---

to growl – knurren, brummen; toad – Kröte

me. I swore to myself that I'd never shed a single tear ever again in my whole life.

After I'd spent five minutes bombarding my face with ice-cold water, I could make out its shape again. Nevertheless, I still looked as if I'd been one of Frankenstein's victims during the night, and that he'd quickly made me a new face out of a couple of old cloths. There was no way I could go out like that.

I rummaged around in Mum's sponge bag, found with some relief her anti-**wrinkle** cream, and read the instructions on the tube. *Smoothes wrinkles. Firms the skin. Reduces swelling*. Perfect! That was exactly what I needed now. I immediately took a whole pile of it and spread it across my face.

Nothing happened. I focused on the mirror, but my skin didn't want to slip sideways or upwards, never mind look less swollen. It didn't move in the slightest. I **smeared** another helping onto my cheeks. No wonder old women get old, I thought, regardless of how much of this stuff they smear on; it's absolutely useless. But then I felt something.

"Ow!"

Suddenly my whole face began to tighten, **itch** and burn. I panicked. That stuff was in the process of turning me into a skeleton. So how was I supposed to convince Simon that I was completely worth falling in love with if I consisted of nothing but bones? I rubbed like mad at my face, and lathered it for a while with soap until the very last remains of the wrinkle cream had gone.

---

wrinkle – Fältchen; to smear – schmieren; to itch – jucken

I barely dared to look in the mirror again. How much of me would there be left? Cautiously, I peeped firstly with one eye. I could at least still recognize the shape of my face. But when I ventured to open the other eye, too, I was **thunderstruck**.

My skin had turned the colour of pepperoni. Just like a big red jellyfish. I looked as if my entire life were embarrassing and the **flush** of shame had decided to become a permanent state. I looked like Finn did after a five-minute screaming fit. There was no way I could leave the bathroom like this. What could I do?

I looked around in a panic and spotted Mum's make-up. Okay. I had no idea how much of this make-up stuff you needed to overcome a disaster like the one on my face. I decided that a handful would be enough.

I felt as if I were in an art lesson. Centimetre by centimetre, I covered my face with beige until no more red could be seen. Mum normally put powder on over her make-up. I wanted to do everything right, reached for the **powder puff** and **wiggled** it around madly in the **powder compact**. A gigantic cloud of dust **shrouded** the bathroom, and I had to sneeze violently. Once the fog had lifted I looked at myself, satisfied. Yes, that would be okay.

---

thunderstruck – wie vom Blitz getroffen
flush – *hier:* Erröten; powder puff – Puderquaste
to wiggle – wackeln, hin- und herwedeln
powder compact – Puderdose
to shroud – (mit Nebel usw.) verhüllen

On the way Jan had given me a couple of sidelong irritated looks, but he hadn't said anything. I hoped that meant that he hadn't noticed my masquerade and that nobody else would either. Especially not Simon. I wanted **to cut a good figure**. I wanted to prove to him that I wasn't a Terminator. Nor **a dead loss**.

When we arrived at the basketball **court**, my legs immediately gave way. What was wrong now? Had the anti-wrinkle cream eaten its way into my central nervous system?

The next moment I had to admit to myself that I wasn't the victim of poisoning but that the sight of Simon, and that alone, had turned my legs to jelly. He wasn't wearing a T-shirt, and his upper body glistened in the sun. He jumped up to the basket like a young god, using all the muscles that a boy's body possesses. I'd never noticed that there were so many of them.

It's not just the back of his head, it flashed through my mind. It's ... it's ... just everything. From head to toe. I threatened to melt like soft ice-cream, and quickly shook myself awake. Pull yourself together! You need your legs! You need your head. You have to play basketball now!

Simon came up to us. "You're here at last."

"We're here at last," I echoed.

God, how stupid!

---

to cut a good figure – gut aussehen
a dead loss – *hier:* ein hoffnungsloser Fall
court – *hier:* Platz

Apart from Simon there were two more boys and one girl there. I had decided at first sight that I didn't like the girl. She had ludicrously long hair which she could have wiped her bottom with, and a nose that was so **dainty** that she could in fact have done without one altogether. There was no way anyone could smell anything with that, never mind breathe with it. And her clothes! Why on earth was she wearing a **crop top** for sport? Were we supposed to be in a modelling competition?

The boys looked reasonably sporty and had no other striking characteristics.

Simon divided up the teams. "Piet, Florian and Lana in one team. Silvie, Jan and me in the other. Let's go."

Simon could not have given me a clearer **rebuff**. He wanted nothing to do with me; he didn't even want me in his team. But what had I expected? Model versus Terminator: so who was likely to win the prince's heart?

I had to get a serious grip on myself to stop the corners of my mouth slipping down onto the ground next to my feet. I felt completely done for, as if I'd had fourteen days of flu with a temperature of forty degrees, or as if I'd had lived without vitamin C for the last three years.

Piet and Florian **surveyed** me critically from head to toe.

---

dainty – zierlich
crop top – kurzes Oberteil; rebuff – Abfuhr
to survey – *hier:* mustern

"You can play basketball, can't you?" Florian asked sceptically.

That was all I needed. In any case, I already felt like a worm that someone had trampled to death. And then along came this **half-wit** and doubted my sporting qualities!

"Fasten your seatbelts," I said curtly.

I'd show them! Simon above all. I was good. I was even very good. I almost always scored and was as quick as a weasel. If there was one thing I could do, it was play basketball. An invisible shot of vitamin C pumped new life into my muscles. I was ready.

"Are you blind?" Florian barked at me.

I had somehow not realized that the game had started, and I'd completely failed to see that Piet had passed the ball to me. But was it my fault that Simon had poured a bottle of water over himself and that the droplets were glistening so confusingly on his body? That was a foul. That was deceiving and distracting the opponent. It was a **fix**!

"She's pretty blind," laughed Simon. "She mostly has her eyes completely shut."

Grr!! Your eyes will pop out of your head! I thought. I did my best. I ran for my life. I battled. But somehow there was something wrong. I didn't score a single goal. It was if someone were steering the ball away from me the moment I had it in my hands. Somehow Simon was always in the way, and somehow the very sight of him made the strength slip away from my arms every time, and the ball flew off

---

half-wit – Schwachkopf; fix – *hier:* Schiebung

wherever it wanted. I'd barely won it back when Simon got it off me again with no effort. It almost seemed as if I were giving him the ball of my own free will. Here, please, take it if you'll like me in return.

I'd never experienced anything so terrible. It felt as if my will had slipped out of my head. And the more of an effort I made, the worse it became. Piet and Florian had already given up moaning at me; they were exchanging irritated looks and after ten minutes of catastrophic basketball, simply stopped passing the ball to me. Oh great! What was I supposed to do now? I tried calling for the ball and getting into space.

"Here! I'm here!" But it was no use. I'd **squandered** my chance. If I'd been Piet or Florian, like hell would I have carried on entrusting the ball to me. Nevertheless, I carried on running. To and fro across the court. I was sweating like crazy. And in my head was pounding: **disgrace**! Disgrace!

Jan, Simon and Silvie were a dream team. They played as if they'd been playing together for years. Thanks to his height and his many muscles, Simon was unbeatable. Jan was a fantastically good player anyway. And that Silvie. Damn. She was just brilliant. A damn model who played basketball like a pro. Not that she'd have been even the slightest bit better than me under normal circumstances. But she had the **pesky** advantage of not having completely lost control over her body.

---

to squander – verschwenden; disgrace – Blamage
pesky – verdammt

I was incredibly happy when the misery finally came to an end. Simon, Jan and Silvie **won hands down**. And I fell into a deep hole.

"Normally ..." I tried to justify myself to Piet and Florian, but they didn't even let me say a word.

"Yeah, right," **grouched** Piet. "Go **knit**!"

Please, dear Terminators up there in the galaxy, come and fetch me in one of your spaceships. I'm one of you. And I can't possibly stay here on earth for a single second longer.

Jan gave me a **punch** on the shoulder. "It wasn't your day. Don't let it bother you."

He meant well, but I couldn't bear that now. Jan wanted to put his arm round my shoulders but I didn't let him.

"Leave me alone!"

"We should play as a team more often."

Silvie couldn't stop reminding Jan that they'd won together. She giggled and cackled the whole time.

"What now?" asked Simon.

"Swimming," said Jan. "I'm completely soaked in sweat."

I just crept along after them, my gaze fixed on the back of Simon's head, which was like a **buoy** without which I'd probably have completely lost my sense of direction. What was going on in the back of that head at that moment? Was he thinking about

---

to win hands down – haushoch gewinnen
to grouch – murren; to knit – stricken
punch – Faustschlag; buoy – Boje

Silvie? Was he thinking about how brilliantly she'd played basketball? Was he wondering how and when to confess his love for her?

"What's that stuff on your face?" Silvie was giving me an irritated look.

"What?"

"There's some **mush** stuck to your face."

I reached for my cheek and, to my horror, found a **batter-like sludge** on my fingers. Oh God. The three tonnes of make-up had dissolved through all that sweating, and had turned into fresh cement.

"That's how you wear it nowadays," I snapped, getting control over my legs, overtaking the boys and throwing myself clothes and all into the tide.

I rubbed the sludge off my face like a mad person. Disgrace! Disgrace! shot through my head. Should I just stay crouching in the sea and never return to land? Perhaps you grew **flippers** if you were in contact with sea water for long enough. And if I had flippers, I'd just live as a Terminator-**mermaid**. Maybe some sperm whale would take pity on me and fall in love with me.

When I did return to the shore after all, Simon was standing before me in all his glory and looking at me, shaking his head.

"You really are **as hard as nails**," he said, then walked past me into the water.

He was right of course. Whilst Silvie was **strut-**

---

mush – Brei; a batter-like sludge – ein teigartiger Schlamm
flipper – Schwimmflosse; mermaid – Meerjungfrau
to be as hard as nails – ein zäher Typ sein; to strut – stolzieren

ting into the water in a totally gorgeous bikini, I was standing on the shore like a wet poodle in shorts and a T-shirt.

Whilst all the others were completely normal teenagers, I had sludge forming on my face, forgot from one minute to the next what a basketball basket was, and threw sausages around. Terminator. Definitely. Hormone-contaminated Terminator.

"You're so quiet. What's the matter?" asked Jan in such a way that the others couldn't hear. We were lying in the sun to dry.

"Nothing."

"Do you feel sick?"

"No."

"Do you want me to get you an ice-cream?"

"No."

"Chips?"

"No. Just leave me alone!"

Oh great! I'd snapped at my best friend for no reason. He was trying to do something nice for me and I'd bitten his head off. Terminator. Definitely a Terminator.

"I'm going," I said.

"I'll come with you," Jan said quickly.

"No. I . . . I . . . want to be alone."

I simply turned and went. Why stay any longer? To make a fool of myself again? To give them further proof that I was as hard as nails? No thanks.

I dragged myself home, slipped unseen past Mum and Dad, who were just changing Finn's nappy, and crept into bed.

The deal

I couldn't understand myself. Outside the sun was shining, and I was lying in bed wailing and sweating. What kind of **wimp** had these stupid hormones turned me into? Couldn't I think of anything else to do than wail and gnash my teeth? Did I have to be depressed the whole day long because I was turning into a woman? I just couldn't understand it!

I pushed the covers back, stretched myself out, and had a long conversation with myself. "So, Lana, let's just summarize everything. Whether you like it or not, you've landed right in the middle of puberty. Bad luck. You probably thought you of all people would be **spared**. Nothing doing. And what is part of this kind of puberty? You fall in love. So far, so good. But on this planet there are other female beings apart from you. That's called competition, Lana. Competition keeps the market alive, Dad always says. So it's no reason to bury your head in the sand. What about a bit of fighting spirit? Nothing's decided yet! You've still got a real chance! It's like the

---

wimp – Softie, Schwächling
to spare – schonen

Federal Youth Games. Even if you're right behind, you can still mobilize all your reserves and catch up. But there's just one problem. You can only catch up if you're in training. And you're not. You're an absolute beginner. You haven't got the faintest idea how girls behave. You need someone to explain this whole mess to you. You need a trainer. And quickly. Okay, you've got another problem. You're not at home. You can't just take a girl from your class to one side and have her coach you. You have to … you have to … oh my God … you have to do something truly crazy, Lana! You have to enter the lion's **cage**. You have to turn the champion into your trainer."

"Hi."

Silvie looked at me without a flicker of interest, but let me in.

"Hi. What …?"

"I thought that as we're the only girls of our age here, and as we're now something of a **clique**, we could meet on our own every now and then."

Great start, I groaned inwardly. Why hadn't I immediately said: okay, so I think you're totally stupid and wish you'd get lost, but my hormones are driving me to make demands on you in your function as an experienced girl.

Silvie looked at me searchingly. "Are you really always so … so …"

Federal Youth Games – Bundesjugendspiele
cage – Höhle
clique – Klüngel, Clique

"Tense? No. Not at all. I'm having ..."

"Your period?"

"Precisely."

Lie. But for the first time since I'd started my periods six months ago, I was happy that I had them. For Silvie, my periods seemed to be reason enough for my tense behaviour.

She smiled understandingly. "It's not easy being a woman."

If only she knew, how right she was!

She winked at me. "But thank goodness for tampons, eh?"

"Yeah, absolutely," I agreed quickly.

Another lie. In all my short life of periods, I'd never used a tampon. I had a healthy respect for them. And if I was honest, I also had a healthy respect for girls who used tampons.

"Hey, Silvie. So, you're really good at basketball. Are you in a club?"

"Yes."

"So am I."

"Hmm. We didn't see much evidence of that today."

I decided not to go for Silvie's throat, nor to explain at great length that today had been a total exception.

I remained as gentle as a **paschal lamb** and tried to make conversation. "Jan's in the club, too."

Oops. All of a sudden, Silvie's ears went red and she stared at me as if I'd offered her a cream cake.

---

paschal lamb – Osterlamm

"So how old is Jan, then?" she asked.

"Fourteen."

"And what's his star sign?"

"**Libra**."

"What's his **ascendant**?"

"How should I know?"

What were these questions all about?

"So has he got a girlfriend?"

"No, he hasn't."

Silvie's features relaxed. Was the inquisition over now?

"Well, that's something," she said, and **clicked** her tongue.

In the time-lapse something clanged in my brain, and then I understood the situation. Oh my God! Silvie Supermodel **fancied** Jan. I couldn't believe it!

"So what kind of girls does he like?"

Obviously. She was completely mad about him. And after just one single afternoon. It presumably wasn't based on his inner qualities, was it? I quickly conjured up a picture of Jan onto my inner screen and checked the points off. Dirty-blond normal-length hair, green eyes, long eyelashes, skin like a baby's bottom (I did at least know about babies' bottoms), broad shoulders, washboard stomach, muscular legs ... I, of course, couldn't see it, but viewed objectively Jan wasn't a bad catch. But all the same.

Libra – *Sternzeichen:* Waage
ascendant – Aszendent
to click – schnalzen
to fancy sb – ein Auge auf jmdn. geworfen haben

Supermodels falling for him struck me as **odd**. And supermodels falling for him even though the back of Simon's head was near enough to touch struck me as even odder.

"Tell me! Does he prefer blondes? Or brunettes?"

Silvie didn't let up. But how was I supposed to know that?

"Jan doesn't have anything to do with girls ... he's just friends with them."

Silvie laughed herself silly.

"What's so funny?" I asked **indignantly**.

"I know what boys are like. And believe me: Jan's interested in girls. **No two ways about it**."

What did *she* know? Which one of us had seen Jan every day for years? Who knew what was going on inside him better than she knew the back of her hand? Who was the blood brother here? Or, rather, the blood sister.

"I know him a bit better than you do."

Silvie shrugged her shoulders; she seemed pretty sure of her facts. "Whatever, he's really sweet. Could you try to find out what he thinks of me?"

Irritated, I pulled a face.

Silvie put her head to one side and fluttered her eyelashes. "Then I'll help you with Simon."

Damn! Did I have a notice attached to my forehead? SIMON, I LOVE YOU? Or else how could everyone see it – or every female, at any rate?

---

odd – seltsam, komisch; indignant – empört
(there are) no two ways about it – daran kann kein Zweifel sein

"Erm ..."

"So, what do you say? We'll help one another. We women have to stick together."

Ah well, what could I say against that? I did in fact need Silvie's help. I had, however, not expected to have to return the service. But if you looked closely at the situation, I had every reason to be pleased. If Silvie wasn't interested in Simon, I didn't have to get her out of the way. Then I could put all my energy into making up for lost training time.

"**It's a deal.**"

Silvie poured us a cola and clinked glasses with me. "Have you ever kissed anyone?"

I choked, had to cough, and shook my head.

"Never?"

"No, never." If only she knew that I hadn't even had hormones until a couple of days ago. "Have you?"

"Of course."

Of course. Stupid question. Of course she'd kissed someone. She even used tampons.

I decided not **to beat about the bush** any longer. "I think I'm not so ... erm ... expert when it comes to ... well ... female **refinements**. I ... erm ..."

"You behave like a boy."

Thanks! I couldn't have put it better myself.

"You're a bit too much like a **builder**," Silvie **mused**, frowning now.

It's a deal. – Abgemacht.
to beat about the bush – um den heißen Brei herumreden
refinement – Raffinesse; to muse – sinnieren
builder – Bauarbeiter

"Terminator," slipped out of me.

"Well, it's not quite that bad." Silvie **scrutinized** me. "You're actually quite pretty. Slightly longer hair would suit you."

"I was going to grow it anyway."

I couldn't believe what I'd just said. Does the advent of hormones make you lose all your principles?

Silvie clapped her hands, keen to start. "So. First things first: the way you walk."

"What do you mean, the way I walk?"

"Builder."

"I think the way I walk is fine!"

"Do you want Simon to be interested in you or not?"

Yes, I did. I pulled myself together and took a deep breath. Whatever the cost. So far as I was concerned, then: the way I walk, too!

"Okay, then."

And then Silvie spent half an hour strutting up and down in front of me. And before she'd completely despaired, I'd understood how girls walked.

---

to scrutinize – prüfend ansehen

A secret poet

"Is there something wrong with your foot?" Mum asked in passing when I got home.

I didn't answer. She'd soon get used to my new way of walking.

"I'm hungry."

"Food's on the table."

Mum had saved me the leftovers from supper. I stuffed my mouth full. This becoming a girl business was damned exhausting and obviously used up masses of calories.

Jan was sitting on the veranda, writing something. I sat down opposite him, a **chop** in my hand. He immediately hid the piece of paper in his trouser pocket.

"So what secret thing are you writing?" I asked curiously.

"So what did you want with Silvie?" he countered.

"Women's things. So, what have you been writing?"

"Private things."

---

chop – Kotelett

Well, that was a very **profound** conversation. I tried to say something funny, but couldn't think of anything. An uncomfortable silence **reigned**, and I asked myself what was wrong. Since I'd known Jan, we'd never run out of conversation. And if we sometimes didn't say anything, the silence had never been uncomfortable. However, we'd never had secrets from one another either. I wondered if I should ask him what he thought of Silvie, but I didn't get that far.

"Is everything okay between us?"

"What could be wrong?"

"Don't know."

"Nor do I."

"So there's nothing wrong."

"Exactly. Nothing."

The conversation wasn't exactly becoming more profound. And the silence wasn't exactly becoming any more bearable.

Jan had the perfect answer. He grabbed the basketball and threw it to me.

"Fancy a round?"

"Of course."

At least you didn't have to talk when you were playing basketball, I thought with relief. However, as we scored baskets and sneaked the ball off one another, it kept clattering around in my mind. What had Jan been writing?

---

profound – tief gehend
to reign – herrschen

When Jan had disappeared into the bathroom for a shower, I crept into our room and rummaged around in his jeans for the piece of paper. Nothing. I looked in his bedside cabinet and in the wardrobe. Nothing. Just as I was lifting Jan's mattress up, Mum came into the room.

"What on earth are you doing?"

"Airing it. Jan's always **farting** into the mattress."

Mum laughed with disbelief. Then she held something out to me. "This was under Finn's fleece."

I took the note from her hand. Jan's piece of paper. Curiosity tugged at me like a **rabid dachshund**.

Barely had Mum left the room when I unfolded the piece of paper and read with growing disbelief.

Your hair is as soft as wool,
I like you like mad.
Your eyes shine like the stars.
I like you so much.
When you play basketball like a star,
I find you simply wonderful.
All girls should be like you.
But I'd like to have you all to myself.
How on earth can I tell you?
I can't just ask you.
You'd be sure to laugh.
I don't want to make a fool of myself.

---

to fart – furzen
rabid – tollwütig
dachshund – Dackel

I was thunderstruck. Was it possible? Hadn't I just sworn blind to Silvie that Jan wasn't interested in girls? So much for blood sister and blood brother: you could still get it wrong. Hormones made it possible! Jan was in love.

I had to sit down. Somehow my legs had gone **wobbly**. Jan was writing love poetry! That was such a mad development that my head spun. And this poem was also incredibly lovely. You could have sent it off somewhere and it would have been published, guaranteed.

I immediately read it once again and shook my head in disbelief. No wonder things were strange between us, I thought. We were both madly in love. Me with Simon. Jan with Silvie. And neither of us had wanted to tell the other. With so many secrets, a peculiar silence could well arise.

I read the poem for a third time and had to sigh the whole time. In contrast to me, Jan had it damned good. Silvie was in love with Jan and Jan was in love with Silvie. He was having everything presented to him on a silver **platter**. He didn't need to spend hours training. God, life was unfair! Why couldn't Simon write me poems like that? But what sort of poems would they be?

When you miss a goal, my heart ***wells up*** *with love?* Or: *My heart beats for you as the sludge drips off your face?*

---

wobbly – wackelig
platter – (Servier-)Teller
to well up – sprießen, aufblühen

To **inspire** poetic outpourings **in** a boy, you had to be like Silvie. To have a way of walking. To use tampons. To possess long blonde hair which you can push behind your ears. Terminators, however, didn't have poems dedicated to them.

I heard Jan whistling in the shower. He sounded the same as ever, yet everything was different. I most probably had to come to terms with the fact that as of now, I would no longer be Number One in his life. The idea that from now on Jan would prefer to play basketball with Silvie hurt a bit, but at the end of the day I would also prefer to play basketball with Simon if I were ever again in the position to play basketball in Simon's presence within the next hundred years.

If only Jan knew what I knew, I thought. It was somehow right that I, as his best female friend, should be the one to tell him the glorious news.

First off, I rehearsed my big entrance. "Jan, your feelings are **reciprocated**." Or, better: "Jan, you won't believe it, but your beloved loves you, too." Or even better: "Jan, there's an end to your suffering because you won't make a fool of yourself."

I heard the key turn in the bathroom lock. Jan came into the room with wet hair, and almost ran straight out backwards. His face looked as if he'd witnessed the end of the world.

He pointed to the piece of paper in my hands and stammered, "You-you-you've read i-i-it?"

---

to inspire sth in sb – bei jmdm. etwas anregen
to reciprocate – erwidern

"Yes, Mum found it. It's lovely."

Jan's eyes suddenly glowed. "Do you really think so?"

"Yes, very much so. You could just have shown me of your own free will."

Jan looked at me as if he'd never seen me before. Somehow he almost looked a bit gaga. "And you're not . . .?" he asked, without finishing his sentence.

"**Jealous**?" I suggested. "Oh yes, I am a bit." I grinned and punched Jan in the ribs. "But love and friendship are two separate things after all. And the fact that you love Silvie doesn't mean that I can't carry on being your best friend, does it?"

Jan didn't reply, but stared at me, confused.

"Does it?" I asked again.

"Silvie?" stammered Jan.

Oh dear. Hormones seem to have an even more disastrous effect on boys than on girls.

"Yes, I can see why you like her," I said sympathetically. "She's a proper girl. Not a Terminator like me. But I'm becoming a proper girl now as well." To prove it, I took a couple of steps with my new way of walking. Now I didn't want to have any secrets from Jan any more. He should also know the state I was in. "And then Simon might write me a lovely poem like that."

"Simon?"

Love really did seem to have hit Jan right in the linguistic centre.

---

jealous – eifersüchtig

"Yes, do you think I stand a chance with him? If I make a real effort?"

"Chance?"

"It's funny, isn't it? It hits us both at the same time. When I could have sworn that we'd be spared all this love stuff for ever. Oh well, that's what all these hormones can do."

I laughed. Jan didn't. Just wait till I tell you the good news, I thought. Then you'll never stop laughing.

I put myself in position and cleared my throat **unctuously**. "Jan, I have to tell you something ..."

But I didn't get the chance.

"I don't want to hear it," snapped Jan. He turned and just left me standing there.

The **impertinence**! What was his problem? That really was too much. If Silvie was now the number one in Jan's life, then Silvie could worry about Jan's moods. For my part, as of this minute, I was no longer at his disposal. That really wasn't my responsibility. I puffed with indignation.

"Find out for yourself that Silvie's madly in love with you," I mumbled. "I don't care whether you're happy."

---

unctuous – salbungsvoll
impertinence – Frechheit

Risking a fat lip

I didn't say a word over breakfast. Jan didn't say a word either. Mum and Dad exchanged countless looks. But before either of them could ask stupid questions, there was a knock on the door and I stamped off without a thought for my perfectly executed way of walking, and opened it.

"Hi."

Silvie and Simon were standing before me in the doorway. My heart **did a somersault**, and from my throat, unasked for and unhindered, jumped a deep **belch**.

For a moment, time stood still, and I could think only one thought: why doesn't a slimy, **warty** toad just jump out of my mouth?

Simon looked at me, his eyebrows raised with **repulsion**, and Silvie took a deep breath. She probably thought at that moment that all the extra tuition in the world was in vain.

---

to do a somersault – einen Purzelbaum schlagen
belch – Rülpser
warty – warzig
repulsion – Ekel

"We bumped into one another at the beach and wanted to see what you two were up to," she said, giving me a **penetrating** look.

"Oh," I replied **tersely**. I was afraid of opening my mouth for one second longer. Who knew what would come out of it next?

I strutted back to the kitchen in as fairy-like a manner as I could. That wasn't so easy with jelly-like legs and Simon's icy gaze on my back.

"There's a mini-golf course not far from here," Silvie **piped** in Jan's direction. "Do you fancy going?"

We set off on foot. After a couple of metres, Silvie held me back.

"So? Did you get anything out of him yet?"

"No-o, I'm afraid not," I lied. "I **surreptitiously** brought the conversation around to you, but he didn't get into it."

Silvie was disappointed. Like hell would I play **Cupid** for you two, I thought.

"I can't really blurt it out, can I?" I asked innocently.

"No-o, absolutely not. Keep it subtle." Silvie took another deep breath and then adopted a cheerful expression. "And now your turn." She surreptitiously offered me a lipgloss. "Glistening lips are totally erotic ... if you don't belch."

---

to penetrate – durchdringen
terse – kurz und knapp
to pipe – flöten
surreptitious – listig; Cupid – Amor

"Do you think I did it on purpose?!" I snapped.

"You just don't have yourself under control."

Silvie pressed the gloss into my fingers and I smeared it on my lips. Ugh, it was disgustingly sticky. Whatever, I thought. Silvie used tampons and had kissed boys. I had to trust her.

"And then the **pout** to match." Silvie **pursed** her lower lip and looked as if she'd run the risk of a fat lip and somebody had given her a **whack** on the mouth.

I tapped my forehead at her. "That looks completely stupid."

Silvie shrugged. "Men have been into pouts ever since Brigitte Bardot."

I didn't know this Brigitte Bardot, and with the best will in the world couldn't imagine what men could find attractive about monster lips like that.

But there you go. Tampons. Kissing boys. I turned my lower lip out.

"Yes, not bad at all. And now …" Silvie put her head on one side, as if she'd broken her neck, and looked up at me from down below with foolish puppy eyes.

"What on earth's that all about?" I asked uncomprehendingly.

"Haven't you ever seen a love film? They always do it like this."

I didn't protest any longer, put my head on one

---

pout – Schmollmund
to purse – schürzen
whack – Schlag

side, and acted like a terrier who'd had its brain amputated. "I feel stupid."

Silvie sighed. "And then you always have to pay boys compliments. They love it when you **worship** them."

"But that's idiotic." I'd never paid Jan compliments and he'd never complained.

Silvie shrugged her shoulders again. "I'll prove it to you," she said. She reapplied her lipgloss again and strutted up to the boys.

I crept nearer and watched it all closely. Silvie's lips swelled, her head went to one side, and she looked up to Jan as if she were about to bark any moment.

"I'm sure you're a fantastic mini-golf player. Oh, what am I talking about. You're probably fantastic at every sport, what with all those muscles."

God almighty, was that ever overdone! Jan's feelings of love would have to **shrivel up** like a dried-out tulip **bulb**. But nothing doing.

"Oh, I'm not exactly unsporty. But you're not either. What with that figure."

I felt a bit sick. Definitely because I'd not been able to get anything down at breakfast. But maybe also because the two of them found it all so easy, and everything was so hopeless for me!

Lana, what about that fighting spirit? I thought quickly. The trick with the fat lip and the compliments evidently works, so let's get stuck in.

---

to worship – anbeten
to shrivel up – verdörren
bulb – Knolle, Zwiebel

Walking in my perfectly executed way, I got myself onto a level with Simon, put my head on one side and pursed my lower lip as well as I could. Simon didn't even **acknowledge** me with a look.

Compliments! Compliments! I thought forcedly. But what kind of compliments should they be? I couldn't compliment him on the back of his head. That had already gone profoundly wrong once before. Okay, on that occasion I'd just run him over, and hadn't pursed my lips or put my head on one side, but even if I were to do that now, the back-of-the-head compliment would definitely not come across well.

So, what do boys want to hear?

You're so intelligent.

You're so well-dressed.

You've got a great haircut.

You're exactly the right height.

But that was all silly.

When we reached the mini-golf course, I still hadn't said a single word, never mind issued a compliment. I couldn't either. My mouth was full of **saliva**. With a monster lip like that, it was impossible to **swallow** properly.

"Let's play mixed doubles. I'll play with Jan, and you play with Simon." Silvie **winked** at me.

---

to acknowledge sb – jmdn. zur Kenntnis nehmen
saliva – Spucke
to swallow – schlucken
to wink – zwinkern

Simon groaned quietly.

Was that ever awful! The boy whose heart I wanted to win got stomach cramps when he had to play mini golf with me!

Okay, I told myself, now you can show him that you're not a total waste of space. If I'd failed at basketball, I at least wanted to shine now.

Unfortunately, I hadn't expected it to be so difficult to look at my target with my head on one side. I was always the last to get the ball into the hole.

Simon moaned. "Just how blind are you?"

It was enough to make you despair. I watched Silvie in order to see how she **reconciled** the sideways head and playing mini golf.

To my surprise, Silvie didn't get the ball into the hole at all. I didn't get it. If she allowed herself to fail before the eyes of her idol, then at the end of the day she wasn't the right trainer for me. But the next moment I understood that this 'incapable' number was part of Silvie's perfect plan.

"Jan, could you show me how to do it?" she breathed.

Jan readily stood next to Silvie and demonstrated the best way to hit the mini-golf ball.

"Hmm. Is that complicated or what?" breathed Silvie as if she'd been born with an empty head. "Could you help me?"

Without further ado, she stood before Jan, reached for his hand, and got him to hit the ball together with her. In the process she pressed herself

---

to reconcile – in Einklang bringen, vereinen

quite close to him. And when the ball did in fact reach its target in this way, she pressed a kiss on his cheek and celebrated as if she'd won the lottery. Jan turned red.

Damn, she was simply a world champion. Should I now ask Simon if he could give a hand, too? I just couldn't do it. Instead, I carried on trying until the sweat stood on my **brow**.

Simon was boiling. "Buy yourself some glasses."

At the last hole he threw his **club** into the bushes with irritation. "**Grotty**."

Jan and Silvie had won. My neck hurt like hell. My mood was **in the pits**. And as I used the last of my strength to try to suck an ice-cream, the little icy ball landed on my T-shirt with a slipping noise. Oh great, I thought resignedly. I'm grotty and a hopeless case.

---

brow – Stirn
club – *hier:* Schläger
grotty – lausig
in the pits – ganz tief unten

Getting onside using the offside rule

"What should I do?" I whispered despairingly to Silvie.

"Pull yourself together."

"I am pulling myself together. But it's just not working," I **croaked** helplessly. "Tell me what to do. There must be something. A secret **recipe**."

Silvie shook her head, frowned, shook her head again and finally nodded. "Okay. Your last chance. So don't mess it up. Find some topic and act as if you haven't got a clue about it. Then he can **show off**. Boys like doing that."

That was supposed to be my last chance? I'd never realized that boys liked showing off. At any rate, Jan never did it. Or did boys only like showing off in front of girls who weren't their best friends? I decided that it was no use comparing Jan and Simon and that my last hope was to stick to Silvie's advice.

So I had to think of a topic. But there wasn't a

---

onside – *Fußball:* nicht im Abseits; offside – Abseits
to croak – krächzen
recipe – Rezept
to show off – angeben

topic in my brain – just a heap of old rubbish. I wanted to ask Silvie quickly for the ultimate topic, but she was already stuck to Jan's side again, and was busy with her own topic. For better or for worse then, I had to be creative.

The weather?

But why on earth would I have no idea about the weather? After all, everyone could see that the sun was shining. The topic of the weather really didn't give anyone even the slightest opportunity to show off.

School?

Just as stupid. I went to school. Simon went to school. Everyone went to school.

I was just about to despair when I was thunderstruck by inspiration. Yes, that could work! I just had to be bold!

I quickly went over to Simon and started talking to him before my little bit of courage, which was shrinking by the minute, could disappear altogether.

"I don't know what made me think of it, but I've always wondered how the offside rule works in football," I said spontaneously.

Of course, I knew how offside works, but I also knew that boys liked talking about it.

Simon looked at me as if he wanted to shoot me into **the great beyond** with his gaze, but then cleared his throat and began a lengthy explanation of the offside rule.

---

the great beyond – das große Jenseits

I nodded non-stop and tried to look as if Franz Beckenbauer himself were giving a paper on highly complicated game strategies. Simon's voice became more and more animated. He was really getting into his stride. And I was pretending to be really stupid.

"I just don't get it."

Simon picked up a stick from the ground and scratched a football pitch in the dirt with a couple of lines. With a great deal of effort I suppressed a **yawn**, and breathed a few words here and there.

"Interesting ... You know so much ... Wow, that's complicated ... Nobody's ever explained it so well ... Now even *I've* understood it."

This pretending to be stupid was an absolutely magical **potion**. There wasn't a trace left of Simon's **rancour** towards me. He was **beaming** at me.

Boys are so simply made, I thought. They explain the offside rule, and then you're out of the offside position.

"Girls just can't think so abstractly," he said, satisfied.

"True. They're so simply made," I said sweetly.

When we got home, Dad looked at me **sympathetically**.

---

yawn – Gähnen
potion – Zaubertrank
rancour – Groll
to beam – strahlen
sympathetic – mitfühlend, verständnisvoll

"You look done for. You're supposed to relax on holiday."

"I am relaxed," I said quickly, but it wasn't true.

I was in fact completely fed up. After five hours of stiff neck, swallowing problems, and acting **dumb**, I was ready for the sanatorium.

"I'm going in the sauna," said Dad. "Do you two want to come?"

"Yes," said Jan straight away.

I wanted to say yes, too. Comforting warmth would be exactly the right thing for my tense muscles and miserable mind. But I swallowed back my answer. Somehow I didn't want to go with Jan there as well. They could do men's stuff and talk about cars while they were sweating in there.

Jan and I **were** still **at** semi-**loggerheads**. We'd hardly exchanged a single word the whole afternoon. And how could we? Silvie and Jan spent the whole time **cooing** at one another. And at the end of the day I'd had to force Simon to pay me any attention. All the same. I thought Jan still owed me an apology for his stupid behaviour yesterday evening. At least a small one.

With my last remaining energy, I sat down with Mum on the terrace.

"So? How was your afternoon?" she asked.

"Good," I yawned. "But being a woman is damned exhausting!"

---

dumb – *hier:* dumm
to be at loggerheads with sb – mit jmdm. im Clinch liegen
to coo – Zärtlichkeiten austauschen

"Why?"

Why? That was obvious, surely. It may well be that you could spare yourself the head-on-one-side business after fifteen years of marriage, but Mum surely must remember how exhausting it was to start with.

"Because you have to spend the whole time making sure you don't do anything wrong."

Mum looked at me, confused. "What sort of thing could you do wrong?"

"Oh, everything. You can't just look at boys, talk to them, and pull them by saying just what you think."

"You can't?"

Was she deliberately pretending to be stupid?

"No, you can't! It's a well-thought-out system. There's a horrendous amount to take into account."

Mum shook her head earnestly. "Lana, listen to me now: don't pretend to be something because other people might think it's right. You must always be yourself."

What was all that about? Mum really was behind the times! I'd tried 'being myself', and it was a complete flop. Nowadays you couldn't just be yourself if you wanted something.

"Mum, you've got no idea."

Mum shrugged her shoulders. "You have to learn for yourself. I will just say one thing to you: you're wonderful just as you are."

To you, maybe, I thought, irritated. It doesn't matter to you whether I'm a Terminator or not. You're not supposed to fall in love with me. I sometimes wished my mother had a bit more of an idea about reality and wouldn't just see everything through her esoteric rose-coloured glasses. *I'm Okay – You're Okay*, and whatever all those books were called. Someone should take them away from her and show her the raw reality of pubescent girls instead.

When Jan and Dad came out of the sauna, I could barely keep my eyes open with tiredness. That had one advantage. If you were so tired, you weren't quite so much in love. I only had to think about Simon's smile once every five minutes. He'd smiled at me quite often over the course of the day. Once after the offside rule. Once after he'd told me what certificates he'd won in which Federal Youth Games over the last eight years. Once after a detailed account of his last basketball tournament. Once ... I couldn't quite remember. I just knew very well that it was a wonderful feeling to be smiled at by Simon and that I'd do anything to keep having this pleasure over and over again.

"So you're really mad about Simon?" asked Jan when we were undisturbed.

I decided that this question came damned near to an apology, and nodded. "Yes, at least as much as you are about Silvie."

Jan was silent and looked somehow depressed. Okay, I thought, I won't be like that. Silvie's advice was very useful to me today, so it was my turn to do a good deed.

"I know something you don't know."

Jan looked up. "And what's that?"

"Well, it's blonde," I said **pertly**.

"Eh?"

"You don't really deserve it because you're always so foul to me. But I'll tell you all the same."

"What is it?"

"Silvie told me ..." I inserted a dramatic pause during which Jan's eyes almost popped out of his head, "... that she's madly in love with you. If you ask me, that means: you're in love with her, and she's in love with you. According to my arithmetic, there's nothing in your way. Go for it!" I grinned broadly.

Jan didn't. "You mean I should ask her if she wants to ..."

"Of course. It's obvious. Someone has to make the first move. And it's normally the man. She's just waiting for you." My voice sounded as if I'd eaten spoonfuls of knowledge about love.

Jan seemed to be incapable of doing anything at all, from the sheer fact of being in love. Instead of rejoicing like mad at the news, he **nibbled** at his fingernails.

"And you really want that?" he said, completely out of context.

"God, Jan. Who cares whether it's what I want? It's what you want."

"It's what I want," echoed Jan.

"Jan to Earth. It's time you two kissed, or you'll completely lose the plot."

---

pert – schnippisch
to nibble – *hier:* nagen

Dry run

Next morning I woke up very early and was horrendously nervous. A terribly large number of critical things were on the **agenda**. Jan would question Silvie. And what would happen then? Would she kiss Jan? I couldn't imagine it with the best will in the world. Did Jan even know how to kiss?

"Do you know how to kiss?"

I knew from my own experience that it wasn't great to be woken up with such a complicated question, but I was just dying to know the answer.

"What kind of stupid question is that?" Jan pulled the bedcovers over his head and grunted.

"It's not a stupid question – it's a damned important question. You'll have to kiss her, after all. If you're going out with someone, then you just kiss them, don't you? So, do you know how to do it?"

Jan didn't move under his bedcovers. I jumped up and down on his bed until the bed squeaked and Jan was shaken **to and fro**.

"Do you or don't you?" I trilled to the music of *Daylight In Your Eyes*.

---

agenda – Tagesordnung; to and fro – hin und her

That worked.

"God almighty, Lana, you're a **pest**! No, I don't know how to. You know that very well. But it's probably not that difficult. And anyway, who says you have to start kissing straight away?"

My poor Jan! He really didn't have a clue. What else were you supposed to do if you were going out with someone? And how were you supposed to be going out with someone if you didn't do that?

"You're just nervous because you've never kissed anyone yourself and you're wondering if you know how to do it!" Jan fired at me.

That **hit home**. And to my annoyance I had to acknowledge that Jan was right. I dropped down onto the bed with a bump.

"True. We're in the same boat. So what happens?"

Jan shrugged his shoulders. "Lips together, mouth open, tongue out, and then get stuck in somehow," he murmured.

I raised my hand to my mouth and followed Jan's emotionless instructions. Lips on the back of my hand, mouth open, tongue out, and then got stuck in. Within a second my hand was **sopping wet**.

"**Nah**, that's not how you do it."

Jan produced his own hand. "You're being much too slobbery and much too quick."

Jan pressed his lips on the back of his hand and

---

pest – *hier:* Quälgeist
to hit home – voll ins Schwarze treffen
sopping wet – patschnass
nah – *Umgangssprache:* nein, nee

waved his tongue around. That didn't exactly look like Hollywood either. But I copied him all the same.

"That sort of thing," said Jan. For him, this was the end of the topic.

Not for me.

"Jan, you absolutely have to tell me afterwards what it was like," I **nagged**.

Jan went into the bathroom in order to get some peace and quiet from me. I fell back onto the pillows and sighed. All the things you had to know! It wasn't enough to use every trick to pull a boy. When you'd pulled him, you had to know how to kiss as well.

But I'd not got that far yet. And I had the advantage that Jan would in any case get there before I did. And since Silvie already knew how to kiss, she would show Jan, and then he'd show me. Good plan!

It was damned windy at the beach. Mum and Dad went straight back home with Finn. So much wind was far too dangerous for babies. Good, I thought. On the other hand, a real gust of wind like that could simply have carried him to Timbuctoo.

Jan and I erected the windbreak. However, neither of us lay in the sun; instead we looked all around the beach. Where had Simon and Silvie got to?

Instead of our two idols, Piet and Florian came **strolling** across the beach towards us.

---

to nag – herumnörgeln
to stroll – schlendern

"**Duck**!" I snapped. I pulled Jan under the windbreak, and quickly pulled a towel over us.

"What's the matter?" asked Jan, irritated.

"Piet and Florian are coming. I don't want them to see us."

"Oh, well reacted," said Jan.

"Do you really think so?"

"Yes. They're totally stupid."

"They've got about the same amount of charisma as **parking-meters**," I said.

"As **expired** parking-meters," Jan added, grinning.

"As defective parking-meters."

We had to start laughing. And right in the middle of our cackling we heard a **piqued** voice.

"Are you under there?"

All of a sudden, the towel was torn off us and we stared up out of the linen like two captured criminals. However, it wasn't Piet or Florian who'd caught us, but Simon. He looked at us uncomprehendingly.

"We were just practising in case there was a killer gull," I said quickly.

Jan giggled.

Simon didn't. "So far as I know, there's no such thing as a killer gull."

Damn. All of a sudden, I felt terribly silly. I quickly put my head on one side and smiled my most pouty smile. "You're right. There most probably

---

to duck – den Kopf einziehen, in die Hocke gehen
parking-meter – Parkuhr
to expire – ablaufen; piqued – pikiert

aren't any killer gulls. You know far more about these things than I do."

Simon grinned. I had just managed to **appease** him again. Jan looked at me as if he were about to say at any moment: you're not normally **off your rocker**. But he didn't know how hard it was to please a boy. He didn't have such problems. He was a boy, after all.

"I remembered," said Simon, sitting down next to me, "in the last tournament, it wasn't in the sixteenth minute that we scored the **equalizer**, it was ..."

What was he talking about? I couldn't care less when or where he'd thrown whatever balls.

"Really? Oh, great that you remembered," I breathed, enormously interested. "And what happened then?"

Whilst Simon told me which wrong decisions the referee had made and when, and whilst I got terribly worked up about his unbelievable injustice, Jan poked around at a **mussel** with his foot, in a bad mood. No doubt he was sad because Silvie hadn't appeared yet. Or was he worrying about his kissing qualities? Thank God Silvie came **bounding** across the beach at that moment.

"Hello-o-o!" she trilled, waving a piece of paper. "Look what we're doing this evening!"

---

to appease – beschwichtigen
to be off one's rocker – verrückt sein
equalizer – Ausgleichstreffer; mussel – Muschel
to bound – springen

The piece of paper announced a disco that was taking place in the beach pavilion. This evening at 7 pm – for teenagers. Disco? I'd never been to a disco. And to be honest, I didn't have any desire to try it out either. I was about to suggest quickly that we play a round of basketball instead of going to the disco, even though I wasn't sure whether I'd make a terrible fool of myself. But it was better to play basketball badly for a second time than not to know for the first time how to behave at a disco.

"Cool idea," said Simon.

"Fantastic," I said. "Disco sounds brilliant!"

"I think discos are stupid," **grumbled** Jan.

Silvie's face darkened. "Really?"

Jan nodded **obstinately**. My God, was he inept. His beloved wanted to go to the disco, and he outed himself as a **party-pooper**. Didn't he have any idea that this wasn't exactly love-provoking?

"Oh, please!" breathed Silvie. "If it's stupid, we can leave early and do something else. Please, Jan! It won't be any fun without you."

Jan sighed. "If you want."

And, yet again, I'd learnt something else new. Boys had to behave in a different kind of strange way to please girls than girls had to do to please boys.

The day passed in no time with card games, head-on-one-side, and asking-stupid-questions.

---

to grumble – murren
obstinate – stur, störrisch
party-pooper – Spielverderber

"Simon, tell me again what happens when you get a seven?"

When I wasn't in the process of acting dumb, I watched Jan. It seemed that he hardly dared look at Silvie for sheer excitement, never mind taking the initiative.

I wondered quickly whether I shouldn't put an end to the misery by whispering to Silvie that Jan was just as mad about her. Perhaps she might have turned a blind eye and taken the initiative, even though she was the girl and Jan was the boy. But I decided against it. With this information, I held a gigantic trump card. And I couldn't just squander it unused.

I leant down to Silvie. "I've got something to talk to you about." I adopted my most conspiratorial smile. "Just the two of us."

Party Queen and Disco Dork

Silvie tripped excitedly behind me. "What? What do you have to talk to me about?"

I looked at her **sternly**. "I'll reveal all. But first you have to make me fit for the disco. I don't want to make a fool of myself. Believe me, the information is worth it!"

Silvie was now completely wild with excitement. "That's **mean**."

Yes, it really was mean of me. But I remained firm.

When we got to Silvie's house, she seemed to have reconciled herself to her fate and began her lesson in Disco Suitability.

"Well, there are three things of prime importance at a disco evening," she said. "The outfit, dancing, and communicating without words."

"And we're supposed to manage all of that in two hours?" I looked black.

"We've just got do some intensive training. So, make an effort if you don't mind."

---

dork – Idiot
stern – streng
mean – *hier:* gemein

Okay. I'd make an effort. I'd give everything. I'd set a new world record for Becoming Disco-Suitable.

Silvie went to the CD player and inserted a Kylie Minogue CD. Then she placed herself in the middle of the room, **whipped out** her **hair-bobble**, and shook her mane like mad.

"Stop!" I pressed the off button. "How on earth am I supposed to do that? I've not got any hair to shake. Have you forgotten?"

"Then just shake your head." Silvie evidently had no desire to have a long discussion, and pressed the start button again.

I took a deep breath and shook my head as vigorously as anyone possibly could. Could so much shaking lead to permanent brain damage? At any rate, I was already **dizzy** after a few seconds.

Silvie didn't seem to mind the shaking in the slightest. She stood with her legs apart and then began to waggle her **hips** as well. I copied her, and got into a terrible mess. I shook my hips and waggled my head.

"No-o-o," grumbled Silvie. "The other way round."

I tried to concentrate. Silvie paraded around me, shouting out instructions like a born **sergeant-major**.

"Firm **bum**! ... Don't look so tense ... Smile. Smile. Smile."

---

to whip out – schnell herausziehen
hair-bobble – Haarspange; dizzy – schwindlig
hip – Hüfte; sergeant-major – Feldwebel; bum – Po

Silvie was probably taking out all her anger on me for the fact that she was still **on tenterhooks** with no information. I couldn't really blame her.

"Don't grin like Kermit the Frog ... Be **seductive** and don't forget your lips. Keep up the lovely pout ... Don't act so stupid."

I pressed the off button. "How on earth am I supposed to take all that in at once?"

Silvie shrugged. "That's your problem. And again! Here we go!"

I shook my head, swung my hips, and showed my lips. God, was this exhausting! Basketball training was a walk in the park by comparison. Sit-ups and **press-ups** seemed to me like **blissful** relief compared with this.

"And now your arms!" yelled Silvie.

"What now?"

It was enough to make you despair.

"Your arms in rhythm. Up. Side. Down. In circles."

After half an hour of Kylie Minogue I had got it. I was soaked with sweat and couldn't get rid of the feeling that I'd never be able to get *I can't get you out of my head* – out of my head.

"So. Next topic. Non-verbal communication."

The way Silvie threw strange words around, **pulling** must be a recognized science, a school sub-

---

on tenterhooks – auf die Folter gespannt
seductive – verführerisch
press-up – Liegestütze
blissful – wonnig; pulling – Baggern

ject, a course of study that you could even do a **PhD** in. Lana Körber, Professor of Pulling.

Silvie sat herself on the sofa. "Imagine the music is deafening. You're thirsty. What do you do?"

"I go to the bar and get something to drink."

"Wrong!"

"I go to the loo and drink from the tap?"

"No!!!"

"I don't know."

"You get your beloved to get you something to drink so that you can thank him beyond all measure."

"Oh. I hadn't thought of that."

"So? What do you do? Bear in mind that words are no good."

I **pondered** for a moment. Then I struck a pose and panted for breath like someone crossing the desert with no hope of an oasis. I took an imaginary bucket and poured it down my throat.

To finish, I took a bow and was hugely proud of my great non-verbal communication skills.

"For God's sake, that's not what you do." Silvie was anything but satisfied with my non-verbal communication skills. "Watch. I'll show you."

With two fingers, she gently stroked her throat, then she made a small slit in her pouted lips and rubbed them gently with her tongue. With a barely **perceptible** gesture she then suggested touching glasses.

PhD – Doktortitel; to ponder – tief nachdenken
perceptible – wahrnehmbar

Oops. That was the difference. I had to admit it. Pretty much the same difference as there was between Romy Schneider the wimp and Arnold Schwarzenegger the Terminator. I did my best to copy it.

Silvie nodded slowly. "That'll do. Next situation."

I learnt to ask someone to dance using shoulder wiggles and a **jaunty** lift of the eyes. I practised gently **fanning myself** to signal that I just had to get some fresh air. And I managed by pulling on my **ear-lobes** and closing my eyes to declare that I would very much like to be kissed.

"Erm ... as we're on the subject of kissing. How exactly ... erm ..."

"How do you do it?" asked Silvie, irritated.

I nodded.

Silvie groaned, but then lifted up her hand, pressed her lips against it like baby fat, opened her mouth slightly, and touched her tongue gently against her skin. It looked incredibly skilled.

"That's how you do it. Next point: the disco outfit. What do you intend to wear?" Silvie asked.

What should I intend to wear? "Jeans and a **hooded** sweatshirt."

"Jeans and a hooded sweatshirt? For God's sake! That's no good," said Silvie, **outraged**.

---

jaunty – flott, keck
to fan oneself – sich fächeln
ear-lobe – Ohrläppchen
hooded – mit Kapuze
outraged – schockiert, entrüstet

"No?"

"No. Then we could have spared ourselves all this practice. You need a skirt and a tight-fitting top."

Skirts were in fact stupid. But at that moment it seemed even more stupid to me that I didn't own one.

"My mother's got a mini skirt. If I use two safety pins, then ..."

Silvie pulled a tortured face. "Okay. Your mother's mini skirt. Shoes?"

I mentally went through all my shoes. Nikes. Adidas. Kangaroos. "I've only got trainers."

"Oh dear. What size?"

"38."

Silvie went into the hall and came back with a pair of Ballerinas. "They're size 37. Just don't wear them out."

I slipped the shoes on to try them out, and immediately felt like **Cinderella's** ugly sister, **faking** it as the beautiful princess. Please, please, dear God, don't let Prince Simon notice that there's blood in my shoes!

Silvie pulled me after her into the bathroom. "Sit down!"

I obediently took a seat on the loo.

Silvie squirted half a tube of gel into her hand and rubbed it around on my head.

"If you've not got long hair, then you can at least have a wet look," she said, quite the hair stylist.

Cinderella – Aschenputtel
to fake sth – etwas fälschen, sich ausgeben als

Then she grabbed a tin of powder and was about to get stuck into me.

"No!" I rebuffed her vigorously. I'd had enough experience of powder and sweat-producing physical activity.

"Then at least cover up the **blackheads** on your nose."

Blackheads on my nose? I didn't have blackheads on my nose. I stared into the mirror. "I can't see anything."

"You have to get closer. Or wait. Take this." Silvie pressed a magnifying mirror into my hands.

When I looked into it, my face distorted like in the hall of mirrors at the fair, and my nose came towards me. And then I saw them. Blackheads. An entire horde of small **greedy** parasites had gathered on my nose.

"How did they get there?"

Silvie sighed. "You want to get as close to Simon as you are to the mirror, don't you?"

Of course I wanted to.

"Then those things have to be covered up!"

I accepted that. Silvie smeared **concealer** on my nose which, I thought, didn't entirely match my skin colour. But I didn't say anything. Better to have a mixed-tint face than dirty little creatures in my pores.

"Ready. And now your information!" Silvie put

---

blackhead – Mitesser
greedy – gierig
concealer – Abdeckcreme

her hands on her hips. She evidently didn't want to wait a second longer.

I spat it out. "Jan fancies you."

Silvie stood with her mouth open.

"Really?"

"Yes, really. He's mad about you."

"How . . . ?"

"I know. After all, he's my best friend," I said sternly.

I wondered briefly if I should tell her about the poem, but decided against it. I didn't want to spoil things for Jan.

Silvie emitted a cry of delight and ran madly to and fro. "Oh God, it's fantastic!"

She was a different person. Normally always the cool one, she was flapping around like a **plucked** chicken.

"Lana! I . . . oh . . . it's just . . . and you're quite sure, too? . . . Oh my goodness! . . . brilliant . . . then . . . yes, what to wear . . . oh dear . . . Fantastic!"

I'll go mad if I don't leave now, I thought. Silvie could stammer and cry with delight to herself all alone. I mean, we didn't want to exaggerate this **bosom buddies** thing. I wouldn't put it past her to fling herself into my arms out of sheer happiness. And I really didn't need that now. And, what's more: it was just before 7.00 and I still had a horrendous amount to do.

---

to pluck – rupfen
bosom buddy – Busenfreund

"Mum, I need you!"

Mum thrust Finn into Dad's arms and followed me into the bedroom.

"We've got to make the mini skirt my size somehow. And I need something tight for on top."

"**Roger**," said Mum, and saluted.

We had to laugh. Mum turned out to be a genius when it came to making things fit. Instead of safety pins, she made a couple of skilful tucks in the waistband as quick as a flash, and bingo: the mini skirt fitted as if I'd been poured into it. Then she rummaged about among her tops and found one that was in fact too tight for her. It was red, and as if made for the mini skirt.

"You can keep it."

"Thanks."

When I was dressed and ready, Mum smiled like on Christmas Eve in front of the festively decorated tree. "Lovely."

"Not silly?" I asked sceptically.

Mum pulled me over to the bathroom mirror. "See for yourself."

I looked at myself critically. Hmm. Oh. Well ... "Not at all bad," I said, grinning.

Mum nodded. "Sensational, if you ask me. Mr Back-of-the-Head's eyes will drop out of the front of his head."

"I hope so."

Roger – *Funksprache:* Verstanden!

Non-verbal communication

Silvie looked as if she'd just dropped off the **catwalk** when she came to pick us up. She was wearing an ultra-short mini dress made from shimmering fabric, and she had brushed up her hair into a sensational mane. And she was all fired up. I spotted chaotic marks on her neck, and her eyes were glued to Jan, who grinned at her **wryly**.

The beach pavilion where we'd bought our ice-creams during the day had been completely transformed. The windows were darkened, so the disco lights glowed and flashed across the floor. The tables and chairs had been cleared away, and a DJ had spread his equipment out in a corner. The music boomed loudly, and I was glad that I'd taken a crash course in non-verbal communication.

First off, Jan fetched a round of colas for us, without pantomime performances having been required. And I looked around like mad to see where Simon was.

Instead of Simon, Piet and Florian came bursting

---

catwalk – Laufsteg
wry – schief, ironisch

in. Oh dear, that was the last thing I needed. I looked demonstratively in a different direction. Too bad that I didn't have a towel **handy** this time that I could throw over myself like a magic hat to make myself invisible.

After a few seconds I decided that the danger was over. Piet and Florian would surely long since have reached the other side of the room. I turned round and uttered a sharp **shriek** of surprise. Piet was standing centimetres away from me and grinning.

"You look good tonight!" he yelled so that my eardrum shook.

I was just wondering if I should demonstratively block my ears when Jan rushed to my aid. He placed himself between Piet and me with an apologetic smile, and bent down to my ear as if he wanted to shout something into it. I played along, and nodded.

After a couple of minutes our act worked. Piet clearly began to get bored. And after he'd tried a couple of times to grab my attention by waving madly, and I'd acted blind, he finally turned away and disappeared in the direction of the bar.

I thanked Jan with my sweetest smile and then energetically pushed him towards Silvie. After all, he had a mission to fulfil.

I stood around on my own and didn't know what to do. I had nobody to try out my great non-verbal communication on, and there was no way I could think of dancing. Nobody was doing it. Everyone

---

handy – zur Hand; shriek – schriller Schrei

was staring at the dance-floor as if a fantastic show were on offer. Discos really were stupid.

A "Hi!" penetrated my ear indistinctly through the beat.

Simon was standing in front of me. Had I just been thinking that an evening at the disco was stupid?

My lips formed a "Hi" in return.

I quickly made my half-full cola glass disappear behind me. After all, how was I supposed to pull off the dry-throat number with a glass in my hand?

To start with, though, I pulled nothing off, but instead stared at the empty dance-floor again. It was as if I could feel every cell in my body, and every cell somehow seemed to be bent and **crooked**. I desperately tried to seem relaxed, but my body turned into a single formless knot before my inner eye. A ridiculously dressed, hormone-plagued knot with blackheads.

Suddenly, Simon waved his hands in my direction, pointed to his **thigh**, pointed to mine, and put his thumb in the air approvingly. Oh my God. That didn't come up in my course on non-verbal communication.

What on earth did he mean? He surely didn't mean I looked like a knot, did he? Could you see my inner world so clearly by looking at me? I shrugged my shoulders helplessly.

Simon made a triangle shape in the air and point-

---

crooked – krumm
thigh – Oberschenkel

ed to my legs again. Heaven help me, what could he mean? Was I **knock-kneed**?

Simon came right close and yelled in my ear, "Great skirt!"

Woosh: the knot loosened. The blackheads retreated, defeated, into my pores. All of a sudden, I felt bursting with self-confidence. I was wearing a great skirt!

I couldn't let this great moment pass by **unexploited**. I decided to try the dry-throat number. A gentle stroke across the throat, a lick of the lips, and a sip from an imaginary glass. And how about that: Simon immediately understood.

His lips formed the word C-O-L-A? I nodded, and Simon disappeared in the direction of the bar.

I looked around for Jan and Silvie. Silvie was just pulling Jan onto the dance-floor. Oh my God, I thought, Jan can't dance. He hasn't **enrolled** for a crash course in Disco Suitability. He'd make a terrible fool of himself, no doubt about it!

Silvie got stuck in. Her hair flew around Jan's ears, her hips twitched, and her arms went up and down. Jan stood in front of her, undecided, and desperately tapped his foot in time to the music. But then Silvie took him by the hands and **twirled** him all over the place. Jan could do nothing other than fit in with her rhythm. However, he didn't look happy about it.

---

knock-kneed – x-beinig; unexploited – unausgenutzt
to enrol – sich einschreiben lassen, teilnehmen
to twirl – drehen, zwirbeln

Barely had the song finished than he raced off the dance-floor. He probably felt like a knot now, too, I thought. I felt terribly sorry for him. I absolutely had to encourage him.

Unnoticed by Silvie I stretched out my arm and pointed to the exit. Jan immediately understood, and trotted behind me like a good boy into the fresh air.

"Damn it, Jan. That's not how it works. You have to have faith in yourself. Silvie is just waiting for you to do something. Everything's difficult to start with. But you're in love, so follow your feelings. Ask her! Don't wait any longer. It's your big moment!"

Jan looked at me doubtfully.

"If I had as good a hand as you do, I'd put all my cards on the table straight away!" I said excitedly.

"Would *you* kiss me?"

Poor Jan, what on earth was wrong with your self-confidence? Wasn't it enough that Silvie idolized him? Why did he think he wasn't worth kissing despite that?

"Honestly, Jan! Of course, I'd never kiss you. That would be abnormal. But if I were Silvie, there's nothing I'd rather do than kiss you. Got it?"

It somehow seemed to me as if Jan's shoulders were sinking a couple of centimetres into the depths. That was probably because his knot was finally loosening.

"Okay, I'll do it," he said as if he'd just decided to commit hara-kiri, and **stomped** back into the disco.

---

to stomp – stapfen

Phew! That was done. I hurried behind him so that I didn't miss a single thing.

Jan **steered** himself over to Silvie like a rocket and shouted something in her ear, whereupon Silvie put her hand to her mouth in delight and nodded vehemently. Then they stood opposite one another undecidedly for a moment. Finally Silvie pulled Jan to her and pressed her lips on his mouth. And voilà! There it was: Jan's first kiss.

Somehow I just couldn't turn my gaze away from the pair of them. What was he feeling right now? And would he stay with Silvie for ever? Would they get married? Would he still be my best friend? Would I always have to meet Silvie and say that she was my friend?

All these questions made my stomach feel quite **queasy**. Maybe I was just jealous. Jealous because Jan was being kissed, and I wasn't.

The kiss must already have lasted for a whole minute. When I was finally able to turn my gaze away from the pair, I saw that Simon was standing next to me with two glasses of cola.

Had he been standing there long? Had he seen the way I was staring at Silvie and Jan?

I pointed with my finger to Jan and Silvie, and kissed the air. Simon nodded, grinning, gave me a cola, and stuck his thumb up. He evidently thought that kissing was a good thing in general. That was at least something.

---

to steer – steuern, lenken
queasy – unwohl

For the rest of the evening I did my best to elevate myself to the circle of those who had been kissed. And in fact, everything was going well so far. Simon kept bringing me colas. And I had a permanently bursting **bladder**. He must have grinned in my direction twenty-five times. And I grinned back until my **jaw** hurt. But all the same, I didn't come a centimetre nearer to a kiss. Even though practically everyone around us was kissing. Discos were evidently a complete **cattle-market**. Even Parking-meter Piet had a girl on his arm and was kissing her.

I could think of no other option than to resort to the last of my Disco Suitability lessons. Dancing like Kylie Minogue. I gathered up all my courage and stepped onto the dance-floor. I shook my head and hips wildly, and waited in vain for Simon to join in. But instead, he stayed at the edge of the dance-floor and grinned at me.

I did my best to get various movements into some kind of meaningful order, and kept thinking: please, dear God, don't let me do a **belly-flop** onto the dance-floor now, help me to come across as somehow girl-like.

When I dragged myself back to Simon, completely done for, he gave me a non-verbal round of applause.

Strike! I thought, **rejoicing**. I hadn't made a fool

---

bladder – Blase
jaw – Kiefer; cattle-market – Viehmarkt
belly-flop – Bauchlandung
to rejoice – jubeln

of myself: I'd impressed him. Now he had to kiss me. I stood a bit closer to him and pursed my lips faintly so that I'd be prepared.

But I could have saved myself the bother. I remained unkissed. The whole long evening, Simon made no move, and I didn't dare use the non-verbal communication for 'I want to kiss'. Don't despair, I **consoled** myself. After all, Rome wasn't built in a day, and I had in any case taken a big step closer to my goal.

---

to console – trösten

I want to giggle!

"So how was it?" I asked Jan impatiently after we'd dropped Silvie off at home and Simon had said goodbye at the next corner with a phenomenal smile and no farewell kiss.

"How was what?" Jan grunted back.

"Oh please, Jan. What on earth do you think I mean? I know myself what the air in the disco was like. How was kissing, for God's sake?"

"Quite okay."

"Quite okay? That's it? Quite okay?"

"Yes, it was fine."

"Yes, but what does that mean? Was it fun? Did it warm your heart? What did it taste like? Sweet? Salty? Could you breathe while you were doing it? Swallow?"

Jan gave me a look that as good as said: you've **lost your marbles**.

"It was nice."

I could hear from his tone of voice that he didn't want to talk about it any more. When we got home, he fled from further questioning into our bedroom.

---

to lose one's marbles – verrückt werden

Boys were definitely different from girls. And at that moment I realized again that I was definitely a girl. I wanted to talk to someone about these things. I wanted to spend days and nights listening to all the details about kissing. I didn't want to be alone with all this hormone rubbish. I wanted to be conspiratorial and ... giggle. Yes, it was true: I, who had always thought that giggling girls were mentally defective creatures from another planet, was, all of a sudden, sure that giggling was exactly the right method of dealing with all this whole nonsense. Giggling together with someone would have a **beneficial** effect on my hormones in the same was as warm milk and honey on a cough.

But who should I giggle with? Jan obviously didn't have the remotest desire to giggle with me. I didn't have the remotest desire to giggle with Silvie. So there was only one possibility left if I wanted a bit of giggling: Mum.

I slipped into the living room where Mum and Dad were **cuddling** arm-in-arm on the sofa. I flopped down next to them like a wet sack.

"What's wrong?" Dad wanted to know.

"Oh, nothing."

"You're in a pretty bad mood about nothing."

I looked **pleadingly** at Mum and hoped that she would understand me telepathically. Please, Mum. SOS. Come next door with me and have a giggling

---

beneficial – wohltuend
to cuddle – kuscheln
pleading – flehend

match with me. I need it now. Mum frowned. But after I'd looked hard in her direction once again, my message seemed to have got through. She had got it.

"What would you say to a little evening walk with your old mother?"

I nodded, pleased.

"I'll come with you!" Dad cried in delight.

Oh no, I thought. Anything but that! I rummaged around in my brain for a possible way to get rid of him, but Mum was quicker.

"Weren't you desperate to watch that film on TV?"

Dad looked, irritated, at Mum. "Was I?"

"Yes, you were." Mum's voice allowed no room for contradiction.

Now Dad had understood. "Oh yes, I remember. I really was desperate. Don't be too sad if I let you go on your own."

"We're not!" I laughed, and pulled Mum after me.

We walked along the night beach. Above us was an incredibly starry sky.

"Jan kissed Silvie today," I said to get straight into the topic.

"Oh," marvelled Mum.

"He says kissing is quite okay."

"So that's what he says."

"I somehow thought kissing was more than just okay. But maybe I'm wrong."

"Would you be interested to know how I find kissing?" asked Mum.

I took her arm and giggled briefly to myself. And

without my having to ask her, Mum giggled with me. That felt go-o-o-d!

"Hmm. Yes, I would. Tell me."

"Well, the first time I was kissed, I was ... let me think ... I was thirteen. Like you."

We giggled again. Giggling was a bit like letting **sherbet** dissolve on your tongue. Giggling parcelled up my swirling thoughts about Simon into soap bubbles that gently danced through the air. Giggling set your head free. Giggling allowed you to breathe properly again.

"It was on my Aunt Hilde's 80th birthday," Mum continued. "It was quite late, the adults had **had a few**, and Uncle Paul was singing dirty songs. Yes, and on this birthday my second cousin was there. Stefan. He was fifteen. I have no idea what became of him. Anyway, we hid under the table cloth of the big buffet and listened to what the adults were saying."

Now I couldn't stop giggling. I almost felt a bit dizzy. Like on last New Year's Eve when I had secretly drunk the **dregs** from the adults' sekt glasses and was still **hiccupping** at midnight.

"And then my cousin Stefan seized the opportunity and kissed me without any warning."

"No! What a swine!" I cackled like a hen.

"Yes, quite **brazenly**. Men!" Mum **chuckled** and I pressed my head into her cardigan.

---

sherbet – Brausepulver
to have had a few – einige hinter die Binde gekippt haben
the dregs – Bodensatz; to hiccup – Schluckauf haben
brazen – unverschämt; to chuckle – schmunzeln, kichern

"And what did it feel like?"

"Pretty good! It was somehow quite soft." Mum was now visibly wallowing in memories. "And it tasted a bit like **shortcrust pastry dough**, but more tender. And his breath was quite warm. Almost like a hairdryer. And the down on his upper lip **tickled**. But the nicest thing was that it was something new. I'd never experienced anything like it. It felt quite different from anything I knew."

I sighed. Mum knew which details were important for a woman. "Yes, that's how I imagine it as well. More than just okay."

After a short pause during which Mum was no doubt thinking about her first kiss and my first kiss, hopefully soon to come, Mum giggled again.

"How's it going with Mr Back-of-the-Head?" she asked.

"He keeps smiling at me. And he pays me compliments."

Mum nodded. "But that sounds good."

I nodded.

"When you've kissed him, will you tell me?" asked Mum, with such a curious expression that she looked for a moment as if she was only thirteen herself.

"We'll see," I said sternly, but I knew that I would absolutely definitely tell her everything.

"Are you still having to make such an effort to be different from how you are?"

---

shortcrust pastry dough – Mürbeteig
to tickle – kitzeln

Did Mum have to start with all that again? However cool and friend-like she could sometimes be, however well you could giggle with her, when it came to pulling she was just behind the times.

"No, it's all wonderful, Mum," I said tersely.

"That's good. It's not healthy for the soul, having to bend and **buckle**."

"Yes, yes." I quickly agreed, pointing to the sky and changing the subject. "Look, there's **the Plough**."

Mum followed my gaze. Then we found the **Little Dipper** and Cassiopeia. And suddenly an incredibly beautiful **shooting star** shot across the sky. I'd never in my whole life seen a shooting star.

"Wow!"

"Quick, make a wish," said Mum.

We both shut our eyes. I knew exactly what I would wish for. Please, dear shooting star, let me talk Simon round soon, and let him kiss me, and let it be more than just okay.

---

to buckle – einknicken
the Plough – *Sternbild:* der Große Bär
the Little Dipper – *Sternbild:* der Kleine Bär
shooting star – Sternschnuppe

The involuntary victim

The next day I woke up before everyone else, jumped out of bed, and blocked the bathroom for a whole hour. Mum's mini skirt. Vaseline instead of lipgloss. Water instead of gel. Perfect!

All **spruced up**, I tramped off to the beach on a solitary mission with a determination that **sought its equal**. It had to happen today. After all, I had a shooting star as my ally, and apart from that, I didn't want to wait a day longer. I finally wanted to belong to the ranks of the kissed as well.

I called to mind all the tricks and tips that I'd learnt so far. The walk! Not tramping, but **floating**. The neck. Down with it. The lip. Puffed out!

Simon was already waving at me from a distance. I spread my towel out next to his and stretched out in the sun like a gazelle.

"Oh, Simon, you really are a true man. You're so muscular. And so clever."

---

involuntary – unfreiwillig
spruced up – geschniegelt
to seek its equal – seinesgleichen suchen
to float – schweben, schwimmen

Simon glowed. "At first I thought you were a bit of a **nutcase**. But since then ..." he said, his chest swelling with pride.

"Yes, what since then?" I breathed, and could only just stop myself from shaking him like mad and shouting loudly: kiss me!

I felt as if I were sitting on a **powder keg**. All this gallantry was getting on my nerves. The gentle whispering awoke in me the need to shout out **swear words**. I gently brushed a grain of sand off my knee with my fingers and looked enquiringly at Simon with a perfectly executed puppy-dog gaze.

"Since then I've realized that you're a really sweet girl."

Oh, ye-e-e-e-s! I thought. I felt like butter, and had a serious fear that I could melt away within seconds in the full sun. Then all that would remain of the sweet girl would be a horrible fatty mark which would slowly seep away into the sand. I decided not to melt but instead to grow with pride. I had done it. I now belonged to the league of sweet girls, not to the species of Terminators-gone-mad. And I wouldn't mind helping this image to gain even more gloss and glory. For this purpose, a little sand-fly came to my aid. It hopped onto my swimsuit and seemed to want to sun itself there for a good long while.

"Ugh!" I squealed in a girl-like manner. "I hate insects. They're so disgusting."

---

nutcase – Verrückte/r
powder keg – Pulverfass
swear word – Schimpfwort

I'd learnt that in my class. All the girls in my class thought insects were disgusting. I, however, thought that insects were completely fascinating. When the annual spider epidemic hit our school every summer, the girls were screaming at every spare moment. Disgusting! Those long legs! They're always darting around! And before they could get stuck into the poor leggy creatures with board-rubbers and pencil cases, I always climbed onto the window-sill and reached for one spider after another, stuffed them in a box, and set them free in the school playground.

Sorry, I thought in the sand-fly's direction, we both know that you're not really disgusting.

"There's always something wrong with you girls," said Simon, but you could tell from his face that he liked girls always having something wrong with them. "Don't move. I'll do it."

I looked at him like a helpless **chick** and nodded. Bingo! He had the sand-fly in his fist. But instead of putting it back on the ground a couple of metres away and wishing it a happy life, Simon crushed it between his fingers with **relish**.

"It won't bother you any more."

I was stunned. A **grisly** murder had taken place before my very eyes. Deliberate, unregretted murder! And the worst thing was: it was my fault. I had semi-**incited** Simon to do it. I was an accomplice to

---

chick – Küken
relish – Genuss; grisly – grässlich
to incite – anregen

a murder! I'd made him do it. The poor sand-fly had had to give his life just because I wanted to be a real girl, just because I wanted to be kissed. I felt terrible.

Simon, however, mistook my horror for the belated result of being shocked and disgusted, and before I knew where I was, he had put his arm around me. The arm with the hand which still had the mortal remains of the sand-fly stuck to it. The murderous arm.

"It's gone now," breathed Simon protectively.

What was he thinking? Was he proud of having crushed a small, helpless insect? Did he think it was a heroic act? In the same tradition of princes who freed their beloveds from towers, **slew** dragons, and killed wicked stepmothers? It was just unbelievable!

I was about to start shouting at him. But before I could threaten him with animal protection organizations, the murderous arm had pulled me closer to him and the deadly hand had started to stroke my upper arm. It felt damned lovely. And before I knew where I was, my lips found themselves on Simon's lips.

I focused on trying to maintain my indignation. Think about the sand-fly, I kept saying to myself, but the words lost their meaning. I couldn't think at all any more. Simon opened his lips quite gently. A warm wave flowed through my body. Hmmm!! Wasn't that lovely!

I don't know how long we were doing it for. My eyes were shut. I had forgotten space and time.

---

to slay – erschlagen

And when we stopped sometime after a hundred years, I sighed deeply. “Lovely.”

When I slowly opened my eyes, Jan and Silvie were standing directly before us. Silvie was grinning. Jan had an indefinable expression on his face.

“Now we can have a real **couples** holiday!” cried Silvie in delight, dropping down onto the sand next to us.

---

couple – Paar, Pärchen

Rows!

It was so mad. Just a couple of days ago I hadn't even been a proper girl. And now I'd been kissed and was right in the middle of a couples holiday.

However, a couples holiday was a pretty exhausting thing. Ever since we'd kissed, Simon had never stopped telling me terribly unimportant details about his life. I sometimes felt like a nodding dog on the parcel shelf by the back window of the car. I nodded and nodded. And I made up compliment after compliment. If we hadn't done a round of kissing after every story, I'd never have survived the **strain**. But the kissing made up for everything. It was so wonderful. After every kiss I knew exactly how in love I was with Simon.

Sometimes, when I just couldn't concentrate any longer on Simon's lectures or almost got a cramp in my jawbone from sheer smiling, I just pulled Simon towards me in mid sentence and kissed him like mad. He always put up with it willingly and, after the kiss, simply took up the story where he'd stopped it.

---

row – Streit; strain – Anstrengung, Stress

I also tried a couple of times to enrich the conversation with one of my own stories or by making comments such as: "Oh, I know. I had that once, too. That's when I ..." or: "In our team, we do it a bit differently. We ..." or: "Don't you think that people ...?"

But I never got any further. Somehow Simon managed, inexplicably, to interpret everything I said as an invitation for a new torrent of words. In fact, he liked it best if I said nothing at all, but nodded, beamed, and produced a suitable compliment at the end of the story. When I'd complimented him, he rewarded me with a particularly long kiss, with the added refinement of tickling my neck and nibbling my earlobes. Who could resist that!

Whilst Simon raved about his last Maths test and drew in the sand the curve that he'd calculated, I tried to gather what was going on with Jan and Silvie on the neighbouring towel.

The two of them were simply lying next to one another, hand in hand. How relaxing, I thought **enviously**. But after I'd stared over at them for a while, I had to revise my opinions.

"So!" yelled Silvie. "We're going swimming now!"

Without giving Jan even a chance to contradict, she pulled him into the water with her.

And in the water, too, she took command.

"Take me on your shoulders! ... Swim next to me! ... Splash me!"

When the two of them came back to the shore, it was no better:

---

envious – neidisch

"Rub my back dry! ... Peel me an orange! ... Rub suncream on me!"

Being a couple was an exhausting thing. Ah well. You don't get something for nothing. If you wanted to kiss, you had to learn to live with the other stuff, too. That's just the way being in love was.

You couldn't be **egotistical** any more and simply do what you liked. You had to take account of someone else, fit in, make compromises. After all, a couple consists of two people. If you don't want that, you just have to become single again. And singles don't get kissed. What a terrible idea! I immediately pulled Simon towards me and quickly convinced myself of the sweet advantages of being a couple.

"Being in love is a crazy thing, don't you think?" I asked Jan the evening after next, when we fell exhausted into bed.

We hadn't talked to each other much since the unpleasant conversation about kissing. During the day we were busy being couples, and in the evenings we were too tired to talk much.

"Hmm."

Jan was **taciturn** yet again. This really was starting to get on my nerves. I had once had a mate who **was game for anything**, and now I just had a silent and boring old stick who I couldn't even talk to about our shared experiences. Well, okay, our ex-

---

egotistical – ichbezogen, egoistisch
taciturn – schweigsam
to be game for anything – zu allen Schandtaten bereit sein

periences weren't quite shared. They were more parallel to one another. But you could surely talk about them, couldn't you?

I decided that he wouldn't get rid of me quite so easily this time. "You and Silvie, you get on well, don't you?"

"Hmm."

"Simon and I do, too."

"Hmm."

"He's so entertaining."

Jan finally turned to me. "Oh yeah? Entertaining?" he asked cuttingly.

What was all that about now?

"Yes. He certainly is. Unlike you. It's been like trying to get blood out of a stone with you recently," I said.

Jan sat up and spoke furiously to me. "Then it's a good thing that you've got Simon now and you don't have to waste your time on boring old me!"

"Too right! If I had to rely on you, I wouldn't have much to laugh about." I was really angry now.

"You know what?" Jan snapped at me. "I'm very glad I've got Silvie. She doesn't irritate me the whole day with such stupid questions about kissing or being in love!"

"Oh yeah?" I yelled. "Instead, she spends the whole day ordering you around, your Silvie-Superwoman!"

Jan's face went a deep red. "You can talk. You let that show-off **blather on** at you the whole day!"

"At least he's got something to say. He's had some

---

to blather on – weiterlabern

experiences. He's a real man. He doesn't take the easy way out like you!"

Jan came to an abrupt standstill. "You're just jealous because Silvie's a real woman. She knows what's what. You're just a poor copy of her." Jan walked through the room, wiggling his bum.

What was all that about? Was he **taking the mickey out of** me?

I was about to make a particularly mean reply, but my throat just produced a guttural sound.

Jan paused, gathered his bedding up, and was about to go to the door when my throat did after all produce a couple of **hoarse** tones.

"How could I ever have been friends with you?"

Jan looked at me coolly. "That's what I'm asking myself as well."

For a moment we stared into one another's eyes like two gladiators, both waiting for the other to draw his sword.

Then Jan suddenly turned away from me, went to the door, and slammed it shut behind him.

"**Prat**!" I yelled at the shut door.

But there was no reply.

"Stupid complete prat!"

Nothing.

"Totally stupid mega-prat!"

Then the door suddenly opened.

But it wasn't Jan standing in the doorway: it was my mother.

---

to take the mickey out of sb – jmdn. auf den Arm nehmen
hoarse – heiser; Prat! – Idiot!

In the background I could hear Finn **bawling**, and my father singing his head off: "**Bye Baby Bunting**!"

Mum looked exhausted. "What's going on here?"

"Nothing!" I yelled, grabbing Jan's book from his bedside table and throwing it at the wall.

"But it doesn't sound like nothing. Have you **quarrelled**?"

I just emitted an angry gurgle, and tore the sheet from the side of Jan's bed.

Mum held her hand to her forehead and her concerned look turned to a rather annoyed one. "Lana. That's enough. Your brother has to sleep. So if you don't mind, have a bit of consideration and by all means get angry, but be quiet about it!"

I couldn't believe I was hearing correctly. That was an incredible injustice. "Oh, but when Finn screams the whole night and I can't keep my eyes shut, then that's okay, is it?" My voice cracked.

Mum's face turned to ice. "I really do have a lot of patience. And you pretty much always have the freedom to do as you please. But that's enough, Lana. Your brother has been in the world for just a few weeks. You're thirteen. You want all your freedom because you're not a child any more. But there aren't just rights. There are responsibilities, too."

"I ..." I wanted to object, but Mum cut me off.

"No. I'm not going to discuss this now. You think about it, and for God's sake be quiet." With these words, Mum left the room.

---

to bawl – plärren; Bye Baby Bunting – *Wiegenlied, etwa:* Schlaf, Kindlein, schlaf; to quarrel – sich streiten

I was **flabbergasted**. Nothing like that had ever happened before. My mother had always talked everything through with me. She'd never spoken in a commanding tone like that. But since that little howler had been in the world, that had presumably changed, too. Now she thought I wasn't even worth having a discussion with.

I felt terribly sorry for myself and felt that everybody was treating me unbelievably badly. I cried and imagined being caught by a killer gull. This time it would be fatal for me. And then they'd all kneel around me and tear their hair out because they felt so guilty. Jan would never forgive himself for shutting the door in my face so shortly before my death. And Mum would **reproach herself** for the rest of her life for having stopped my last words. And my stupid little brother would stand by my grave when he was older, and I'd throw **bolts of lightning** down from the sky and ...

I had no desire to think about it any more. After all, I wasn't intending to die. And there were no such things as killer gulls either.

What's more, I had every reason to want to stay alive. At the end of the day, I had a boyfriend. I had been kissed! Why was I getting in a state about Jan and my mother. I didn't need them! I didn't need anyone any more. Now I had Simon, of course!

---

flabbergasted – verdattert
to reproach oneself – sich Vorwürfe machen
a bolt of lightning – ein Blitz

Competition in the discipline of love

When I came out of my room next morning, I saw the whole group of them already sitting at the breakfast table. If any of them thought that I was going to be the life and soul of the party, they'd made a big mistake. I grabbed a bread roll and announced that I was going straight to the beach. I ignored Mum's concerned look, looked demonstratively past Jan, and **cleared off**.

Stupidly enough, it was too early to go to the beach. Apart from a few over-**eager** joggers, there wasn't a living soul there. I crouched on my towel without a windbreak, and tried to feel independent. So this was my new life. The life of a woman. The life of an independent woman. The life of a woman with a boyfriend whom she kissed.

It was somehow rather cold on my first day as a woman without a family and best friend. I shivered, and my teeth **chattered**.

As I was staring with concern at my blue-coloured

---

to clear off – abhauen
eager – eifrig
to chatter – klappern

toes, Jan and my family arrived and erected the windbreak a couple of metres away.

To make matters worse, Mum had brought the thick covers. She waved over to me.

"Come and join us!"

I ignored her. You can't crawl back to me that easily, I thought grimly.

Jan made himself comfortable behind the windbreak without even **deigning** to look at me. I heard him laughing. Why on earth was he laughing? And what about? I thought it wasn't fair that my ex-best-friend and ex-family had anything to laugh about. On the other hand – they could laugh. As of now, I would just laugh, too. With Simon. We would find something that would be tremendously amusing. And then how we'd laugh!

As I was thinking that I already couldn't feel the little toe on my left foot, Simon finally came trotting down the dunes.

I waved wildly to him. I wanted to kiss him on the spot, and to be held until I was warm. And to laugh!

But Simon made for my family's windbreak and made a palaver around it.

"Simon!" I yelled to him against the wind. "I'm here."

Simon waved, but made no move to come towards me. I jumped up, tried with my last remaining strength to preserve a reasonably proper way of walking, and ran to the windbreak without deigning to look at my family.

---

to deign – sich herablassen

I grabbed Simon's hand. "We're lying over there!"

"But I've just been telling your father about the last tournament, and about how I …"

"But you can tell me that."

"But you already know the story."

I knew so many stories that all sounded the same that this no longer mattered.

"I could hear your stories a thousand times," I said in an **angelic** voice, and put my head to one side.

Bingo. The trick simply worked every time.

"Well, in our last game, in the thirteenth minute …"

I nodded and smiled and as I did so, pressed myself as close as possible to Simon in order not to freeze. At regular intervals of ten seconds I laughed out loud.

"No! How funny! Hahaha! That's just too funny!"

The first few times Simon was a bit irritated. "But all I said was that Paul sneaked the ball off me."

"Ye-e-e-s. Hahaha! But the way you tell it! It was just a scream. You're so funny!" I even laughed a bit louder.

And because Simon was so glad that I found him funny, he finally laughed, too. Look! I thought. My life is funnier than yours.

After the story I desperately needed an extra-long kiss. And I got it, too.

In the meantime Silvie had arrived at the beach, had summoned Jan behind the windbreak, and was about to come in our direction. But Jan held her

---

angelic – engelhaft

back and whispered something in her ear. At the same time Simon was about to raise his arm and wave at the pair of them. I stopped him and whispered something in his ear.

"I'd just like to be alone with you for once. Just leave them."

Simon looked at me, baffled, but didn't seem to find my idea too **weird**.

Jan and Silvie sat down twenty metres away on their towels.

Watched by my completely confused parents, Jan and I then delivered a battle of the couples that was quite something. Let's see who's made the better catch, was the battle-slogan.

When I kissed Simon, I secretly stole a glance at Jan and Silvie. Barely had my lips touched Simon's when Jan grabbed Silvie to him.

After quarter of an hour's constant kissing I was really gripped by ambition. If my ex-best-friend hoped I'd give up, he was mistaken.

Simon tried several times to end the kiss. He was presumably desperate to tell me a new thrilling story, but I wasn't having that. I had him firmly in my grasp, and didn't loosen my grip.

It was finally Silvie who made Jan the loser. She well and truly shook him off and wanted an ice-cream on the spot.

I won! I thought triumphantly, and let Simon go.

"Well, you're brutal today," said Simon, unsatisfied.

---

weird – unheimlich, merkwürdig

Whoops! With the competition, I'd quite forgotten to mind how I behaved. And it didn't seem exactly ladylike to dictate to a boy how long a kiss was supposed to last.

I quickly put my head on one side and breathed, "You're just such a wonderful kisser. It must just have got the better of me!"

At around three in the afternoon my tummy was rumbling terribly. I'd not brought any money with me. And Simon was **skint**, too.

Then of all moments, Mum waved across to me and held a chicken leg up in the air. Oh my God. Chicken legs. Crispy roasted. Really juicy inside. My mouth watered.

When I then saw Jan and Silvie moving towards the chicken legs, too, nothing could stop me. I decided to turn my ex-parents back into my parents. Temporarily, at least.

There weren't only crispy roasted chicken legs but potato salad and heavenly cakes for dessert. Behind the windbreak it was at least twenty degrees warmer. Dad even rubbed my feet warm. I had to admit that I was perhaps a couple of years too young to be completely independent.

"Well, is everything alright again?" whispered Dad.

"It's okay," I said tersely.

"Okay's in the right direction," smiled Dad.

After the last crumbs had been eaten, my parents

---

skint – pleite

stood up and decided to take a walk to aid their digestion.

Mum bent down to me. "Remember what I said yesterday. Not just rights, but responsibilities, too. So, look after your little brother, please."

Oh great. You're kind enough to decide to make your ex-parents your parents again, and then you're landed with baby-sitting.

In order not to be tempted to rebel against my 'responsibilities', and in order not to give Jan and Silvie too big an advantage, I quickly **scrabbled** over to Simon and kissed him.

I vaguely heard Dad saying something to me, but didn't get exactly what it was. It was probably some more nonsense like: remember that babies can't **cope with** too much wind. Or: the nappies are in the front right pocket.

What did it matter to me? I had no intention of moving Finn even one centimetre from his place any more than I intended to change his nappies. Never in my life would I touch those revolting nappies!

Simon and I kissed for a long while. But to my astonishment I realized that the kissing was different. It was still nice. It still tasted nice. But more and more, thoughts kept coming into my head that didn't in fact have much to do with kissing.

Should I try tampons when I have my next period? Or: will I be team captain next season? Or: my left leg itches.

---

to scrabble – huschen
to cope with sth – mit etwas fertig werden, etwas vertragen

Without Simon noticing, I constantly scratched my sunburnt thigh whilst we were kissing. And when the kiss had finished, I cast a **surly** look in Finn's direction.

That is, I tried to look at Finn. But I was looking sulkily into empty space.

"Aaarghhh!"

In my stomach everything tightened up as if my **appendix** were about to burst any moment. I just saw red. Like a madman I rummaged around in the blankets in which Finn had been sleeping peaceful-ly.

"He's gone! Oh my God. He's gone!"

My shouting had also ended Jan's and Silvie's kiss. The four of us searched through the blankets, baskets and swimming things. Nothing. In less than no time, tears started to run down my face unhindered. In a panic, I looked across the beach.

"Fi-i-i-i-nn!"

There he was! I couldn't believe my eyes. With giant steps a woman was walking up the dunes. She was holding a bundle pressed to her. Two legs waggled from inside the bundle.

"Stop! Stop! Stop her!" I waved like mad to the fleeing woman. "Follow her!"

I was about to tear off, but Simon held me back. "You can't possibly just follow her. It's much too dangerous. We've got to fetch the police!"

Like a **fury**, I tore myself away, pushing him into

---

surly – missmutig
appendix – Blinddarm; fury – *hier:* Furie

the sand as I did so, and screamed, “So I’m supposed to wait until she and Finn are miles away?”

“Yes, Simon’s right! It’s a matter for the police!” Silvie said decisively.

I didn’t get it. Didn’t anyone want to help me? At that moment a hand grabbed me and pulled me away. Jan!

“What are you waiting for?” he said. “Come on!”

I ran. Indistinctly, I could hear Simon and Silvie calling after us.

“You’re mad!”

“It’s no use!”

Wild pursuit

"Jan! Where are they?" I cried, out of breath.

I could no longer see the woman and Finn anywhere. Had we lost them?

"There!" Jan had seen them. The woman was just getting into a car.

"No!" I cried. "She can't drive off. No! Help! She's got my brother!"

None of the adults around us made any attempt to help us. They simply looked at us, annoyed, and probably wondered why we were disturbing the well-deserved peace and quiet of their holidays. Jan and I ran down the dunes and dived after the car.

"Stop! **Abduction**! Kidnapping!"

We had no chance. The Polo **inexorably** drove away from us.

"Oh my God, Jan! What do we do now?"

I tried to suppress the tears that were burning my eyelids like mad. We quickly looked around. There had to be some solution somewhere!

---

pursuit – Verfolgung
abduction – Entführung
inexorable – unerbittlich

And there was. The solution came **chugging** out of the dunes. A lorry with an open **load area** drove past us. Jan and I exchanged glances and immediately agreed. Follow it! We ran alongside the lorry.

"Jump up!" cried Jan.

I tried to dive up while I was running, but the stupid load area was damned high up. I didn't manage it. I kept trying, and with every attempt my legs became more tired. I found that even running was difficult.

Jan tried from the side. He jumped, pulled himself up, and fell down into the load area. Damn! Why didn't I have that many muscles in my arms? Jan was the crowned King of **Pull-Ups**. In my biceps there was nothing but **blancmange**.

"Jan, I can't carry on. My legs are collapsing!" I wheezed.

Jan leant over the edge of the load space and encouraged me. "Keep going, Lana! You can do it!"

I ran like a madwoman. Was I getting slower, or was the lorry getting faster?

"Lana, you have to get up now. We're nearly at the road, then he'll put his foot down, and he'll shake you off!" Jan cried urgently.

It was true! The lorry had almost left behind it the **traffic-calmed** road to the beach. I had just seconds left.

---

to chug – tuckern
load area – Ladefläche
pull-up – Klimmzug; blancmange – Pudding
traffic-calmed – verkehrsberuhigt

"Jan!" I yelled, completely out of breath. "What should I do?"

"Jump, Lana! Jump as high as you can. Imagine you were jumping up to score a basket. Hold your hands out. Jump! I'll pull you up!"

I was terrified of falling. But I was even more afraid of missing my last chance. Jan held his hands out. His eyes looked at me pleadingly.

"Now!"

I jumped.

Jan grabbed me. My feet lost contact with the ground, swung in the air, and found no foothold. Completely helpless, I **dangled** from Jan's hands, and my knees kept banging against the metal. I was in too much of a panic to feel any kind of pain. I just wanted to find a foothold!

"Don't let go of me!" I cried.

"I've got you!"

At that moment the lorry turned into the road and **sped up**. I desperately searched with my feet for a ledge in the metal that was as slippery as an **eel**. And finally with my left foot I discovered a **jutting-out** screw which I could use to pull myself up.

Jan pulled my hands like mad. With my last remaining strength I heaved myself over the edge and landed on my stomach in the load area.

"Lana? Are you okay?" Jan bent over me.

---

to dangle – baumeln
to speed up – beschleunigen
eel – Aal
to jut out – hervorragen

I quickly checked various parts of my body and couldn't find any serious damage.

"Yes, I'm okay."

Only now did I see that I owed my relatively soft landing to a heap of stinking rubbish. I was lying in the middle of banana skins and old drink cartons.

"You're bleeding," Jan stated, pointing to my knee. He quickly got a handkerchief from his trouser pocket, spat on it, and carefully dabbed the dirt from the wound.

"It doesn't hurt," I said bravely.

Jan grinned at me.

For a moment I felt really good. The air was blowing in my hair, and I'd completely forgotten why I was squatting in the load area of a lorry.

"The Polo!" I remembered, banana skins in my hair.

We climbed to the front over the mountain of rubbish and **craned our necks** to see the road over the driver's cab.

Thank God! There was the Polo. About forty metres in front of us, the lousy **abductress** was driving along with my brother!

"Jan, it's my fault."

"Why?"

"I wished that Finn wasn't there. And now ..." I got no further. The tears **choked** my voice.

Jan gave me a wild look and shook me by the

---

to crane one's neck – den Hals recken
abductress – Entführerin
to choke – ersticken

shoulders. "It's not your fault, got it? It's that woman's fault. No baby has ever been abducted because of fantasies."

I nodded and pulled myself together. After all, guilty feelings and tears wouldn't help Finn. And I didn't have the time to think any longer. At the next junction, the woman **indicated** and turned off.

"Oh, please, let us turn off, too!" I screeched and said a quick prayer.

Why hadn't I wished for free choice about where to turn off when I saw the shooting star? Oh well, I couldn't have guessed that I'd ever want to turn off. But I should have had the sense to credit myself with a wish that I could use for something really important. What was kissing compared to turning off!

An entire **quarry** fell from my heart when the lorry turned off, too.

"My nerves won't withstand this!" I wheezed.

But it became even worse. The lorry got ready to overtake.

"Oh no, we can't overtake!"

I banged like mad on the driver's cab. But it was no use. We overtook. I desperately tried to see inside the Polo.

There she was. My brother's abductress.

"**Witch**!"

Anyone with such a huge, long nose and such **tangled** hair could only be a witch. I'd never seen such a thoroughly evil face.

---

to indicate – blinken; quarry – Steinbruch
witch – Hexe; tangled – verworren

"There! On the back seat!"

Oh my God. A basket was lying on the back seat, and Finn was lying in the basket. The witch had put a fleece over him. I couldn't see him. Hopefully, he was getting air beneath it. Hopefully, he wasn't **suffocating**!

We hung over the **tailgate** at the rear of the lorry and gesticulated to the witch to stop at once. She, however, just waved at us with an evil grin.

"She's as cold as ice!" Jan cried to me.

"Or mad. My God, Jan, she must be nuts!"

"What are we going to do now?"

Before I could even think up an answer to this question, the next catastrophe struck. The witch indicated, waved once again to us with her sly grin, and turned, **hooting**, into a narrow **lane**.

"We've got to get out!" cried Jan.

We hammered like mad on the driver's cab. Was he deaf in there? Why couldn't he hear us?

"He must have loud music on!" said Jan.

Without asking my brain if I might perhaps be tired of life, I pulled myself up on the driver's cab and **braced myself against** the roof.

"Hold onto me!" I cried.

Jan grabbed my legs. "Be careful, Lana!"

I clutched the flat surface and crawled further

---

to suffocate – ersticken
tailgate – Heckklappe
to hoot – hupen
lane – schmale Landstraße, Gasse
to brace oneself against sth – sich gegen etwas stemmen

along until I could hammer on the front windscreen with my hands. That worked. The driver didn't seem to be blind, at any rate.

The lorry immediately slowed down and finally stopped at the side of the road. The driver jumped out of the lorry and ran around madly, swearing at us in Dutch.

"Do you understand German?" I interrupted his torrent of words. "My brother's been abducted. We need help!"

But it was hopeless. Jan and I exchanged a look and decided: we're off!

Without any warning, we sprang out of the lorry like weasels and ran as fast as we could in the direction we'd come from. The driver ran after us, yelling. But with his stomach, which was bigger than my mother's when she was nine months pregnant, he didn't get far. After a couple of hundred metres he gave up running and just swore at our backs.

Soon I couldn't hear him any longer. I only heard my pulse beating in my ears. We ran along the road like marathon runners in line for a medal, until we reached the lane which the Polo had turned into. The lane led across some fields to a piece of wooded land on which there stood a farmhouse.

"Hold on, Finn! We're coming!"

Bonnie and Clyde

"Can you see anything?" I whispered.

Jan cautiously peeped round the corner of the shed that we were crouching behind, out of breath. From here we could see the house. The blue Polo was standing right outside it.

"No. All the **shutters** are closed," Jan whispered back. "We'll have to get closer."

Quietly we slipped from the shed to a tree, and hid behind it long enough for our hearts to beat to some extent rhythmically. From the tree, it was a short sprint to the house. We pressed ourselves, trembling, against the wall.

"What now?" I asked quietly.

"Now we'll creep round to the first window and try to look in."

We stole forwards a couple of metres. I was so busy trying not to make a noise that I stumbled **helter-skelter** into an old metal bucket. It clattered as if someone had shaken out an entire lorry of **scrap metal**.

---

shutter – Fensterladen
helter-skelter – holterdiepolter; scrap metal – Schrott

"Shhhh! Are you mad?" hissed Jan.

We waited five minutes in deadly silence, pressed against the wall, but nothing happened. Nobody seemed to have heard us.

"Come on then."

We reached the first window and I tried to peep through the cracks in the shutters. I suddenly remembered the day when Finn was born. Then I'd had to look through the keyhole. But something had definitely changed: then I'd have given anything not to see Finn; now I'd have given the shirt off my back to see him.

"Nothing!" I whispered. "Just a bedroom. Nobody for miles. Jan, she won't do anything to him, will she?"

"No, she won't do anything to him. What could she do to him?"

"What if she's a cannibal and needed a baby for her Sunday roast?"

My imagination ran away with me. I saw little Finn on a silver platter with a lemon in his mouth and a salad garnish. Tears sprang to my eyes like mad.

"Nonsense, Lana. She's abducted him because he's so sweet and because she wants a child. You know these stories of women who can't have children of their own, so they abduct other people's."

Yes, I knew those stories. And normally, the women in those stories ended up in the madhouse. Please, dear God, don't let her **take out** her madness **on** Finn, I thought.

---

to take out sth on sb – etwas an jmdm. auslassen

We crept further to the next window. This time Jan looked through the cracks.

"The kitchen."

"Quick, see if there's a big cooking pot on the stove," I whispered.

"Lana. Finn isn't going to be cooked. He's fine."

We crept further to the next corner.

"Damn. There's a patio door here at the front. We can't just creep past," Jan remarked.

"So let's go along the ground," I decided.

We threw ourselves onto the ground and crawled towards the patio door. I bravely stuck my head out and quickly looked in. I couldn't see anyone. But I noticed that the door was open a crack.

"We have to go in. She's probably on the first floor with Finn, in the bath no doubt. Who knows what she's getting up to with him ..." I took another deep breath and tried to get rid of my thoughts of white tiles sprayed with red blood.

"I'll go first," decided Jan.

Like **lizards**, we crawled through the patio door that was **ajar** and into the house. I looked around. There was something spooky about the house. The furniture was heavy and dark. The old carpets gave off a **musty** smell. The smell of crimes and madness!

On all fours, we crawled further. A corridor led off the living room. And stairs to the first floor led off the corridor.

---

lizard – Eidechse
ajar – einen Spalt offen
musty – muffig, moderig

Jan cast me a look. Ready? Yes, I was ready. Whatever might await us upstairs, I was ready to **sacrifice** my life to save Finn.

We crept noiselessly up the stairs. Or, rather, we wanted to creep up noiselessly, but the staircase was **ancient** and **creaked** under our feet like in the best horror film. The witch would be sure to hear that! And if she didn't, then all her accomplices would, the acomplices who were just waiting to get their hands on us and preserve us in the **deep freeze** for hard times.

We managed to get to the first floor without being caught.

"You take the left side, I'll take the right," I whispered to Jan.

I didn't much like the idea of creeping around in this house on my own. But I liked even less the idea of **prolonging** the whole thing. I went to the right and peeped into a room the door of which was open. A study. Papers were piled up on a massive desk, and **newspaper cuttings** were pinned to the walls. Oh my God, I thought. This is where a madwoman lives out her madness.

The newspaper cuttings spoke for themselves. They were all articles with photos of babies. She's **possessed**! I thought with a shudder. Possessed by

---

sacrifice – opfern; ancient – uralt
to creak – knarren; deep freeze – Tiefkühltruhe
to prolong – in die Länge ziehen
newspaper cutting – Zeitungsausschnitt
possessed – besessen

the desire for a child. I couldn't stop the sharp shriek that came from my throat.

A second later Jan appeared with panic in his eyes. "Quiet!" he hissed.

I pointed helplessly to the pictures. Jan studied them in detail. When he turned back to me, I could see from his face that I was right.

"She's mad," he murmured.

I nodded.

"We've not got a second to lose," decided Jan.

"But there's nothing up here."

"Then we'll have to go down to the cellar."

The blood froze in my veins. "Into the **crypt**?"

As tense as we could possibly be, we crept back downstairs.

"We need weapons!"

Jan grabbed a walking stick with an iron duck as its **knob**. I looked around for something and saw a long, pointed hat-pin in an old hat on the coat-rack. That would do!

We crept to a door behind which we suspected the cellar steps would be. When we opened the door, it squeaked loudly and penetratingly.

"Damn! Does everything here have to make a noise?"

We didn't let it stop us, and climbed down the cellar steps, our legs stiff with fear. A musty smell of **mould** and wet cloths met us. It became several degrees colder. And it was **pitch** dark.

---

crypt – Gruft, Krypta
knob – *hier:* Knauf; mould – Moder; pitch – Pech

I held tightly to Jan's shoulder so that I didn't lose him and so that I didn't collapse on my wobbly legs. I wasn't normally afraid of the dark. But this darkness was somehow different. Creepy through and through. It was enough to make you completely believe in the existence of ghosts again. I expected a cold **corpse**'s hand to grasp my ankles at any moment.

"Lana, you're trembling," Jan said.

"I'm just cold," I lied.

I felt Jan's warm hand in mine. "I'm here with you."

Yes, Jan was with me. And I'd never in my life been so thankful that someone was with me.

The steps ended in a big room full of **barrels**.

"I don't want to know what's in those barrels," I hissed.

Poison? Blood? Acid?

We could just see that three doors led off from the room. I boldly opened the first one. I'd expected a mummy at the very least to fall out of it. But nothing bad happened. The room just had old household things stored in it. Jan opened the second door. No mummy here either. This was the room with the heating boiler. All good things come in threes, I thought bravely, and **wrenched** open the last door. But there wasn't a room behind this door. There was a passageway.

---

corpse – Kadaver, Leiche
barrel – Fass
to wrench – reißen

"A secret passageway," I whispered.

My hands trembled like leaves, and I was so afraid that the sweat stood out on my forehead. No normal house had a secret passageway. The only houses with secret passageways were those that had a secret to hide. A terrible secret!

Jan put his hand firmly on my shoulders. "We've got to be strong now. If we manage this, we'll never be afraid of anyone or anything for the rest of our lives."

Whoops!

The passageway ended abruptly after twenty metres.

"Oh my God!" I moaned, scratching the smooth wall. "It's a **dead end**. A trap. Someone will have cut off our way back."

Jan tapped me on the shoulder, and pointed upwards. Above us was a **trapdoor**. A narrow ladder led up to it.

"If we go up there, we'll run straight into her arms," I moaned again.

"We've got no choice," said Jan.

He was right. Finn was somewhere up there in the hands of this madwoman. And there was no one but us who could save him. We had no choice!

"Jan, if something bad happens to us up there and I never get the opportunity again ..." I had to swallow. "I just wanted to say: I didn't mean it when I said I didn't know why I'd been friends with you all these years. I ..."

Jan put a finger on my lips. "I know."

Whoops! – Hoppla!
dead end – Sackgasse
trapdoor – Falltür

We climbed up the ladder. With our hands we heaved the trapdoor slightly upwards and stuck our heads through the crack. We were in an old barn. Not in a **torture chamber**. Just in a barn.

"I can't see anyone."

At that moment we heard a noise that made our hair stand on end. What was it? A **chainsaw**? Horrified, I let the trapdoor fall shut.

"Let's clear off!" I suggested. But the next moment I shook my head. "Let's go in!"

"Attack!" said Jan decisively.

"Attack!" I repeated quickly.

We climbed into the barn. Jan held the walking stick in his hand like a sword. I produced the hat-pin and was ready to stick it into anyone who wanted to get at Finn.

We crept forward, always following the noise. It led us out of the barn and into a yard. When we cautiously peeped round the corner, we saw her: the witch!

She was standing in the middle of the yard, her evil eyes hidden behind **protective goggles**, a running chainsaw in her hand which she was using to brutally maltreat a tree-trunk. All over the yard there were **mutilated tree-trunks**. They looked like statues. Statues of children.

Oh God, I thought, shuddering, she's making a

---

torture chamber – Folterkammer
chainsaw – Kettensäge
protective goggles – Schutzbrille
mutilated – verstümmelt; tree-trunk – Baumstamm

wooden figure as a reminder of each of her victims, and soon we'll be standing in this yard as statues, too. Several metres away from the woman I could see the basket with the fleece. Finn!

We stood there with our weapons drawn, and didn't know what to do. A walking stick and a hat-pin were no match for a chainsaw.

Molten lava pumped in my veins, and with one bound I rushed towards the witch. "Hey!" I shouted.

The witch turned round.

"Give him back!" I cried.

The witch switched the chainsaw off. She slowly took her goggles off. Instead of red, thoroughly evil eyes, two big round blue eyes stared at us, confused and shocked.

"I don't understand," she said in almost unaccented German.

Jan **dashed** forward and threatened the woman with the walking stick.

"Fetch him!" he said to me. "I'll give you cover!"

"Children, what …?" asked the witch with the big round eyes, uncomprehendingly.

She's acting dumb, I thought. She's **disguised** her evil eyes with contact lenses so that she looks innocent. But I can see through her!

I thought of poor Finn gasping for air under the fleece, ran off, **pounced on** the basket and grabbed the **shaggy** cloth.

---

molten – flüssig; to dash – rennen
to disguise – tarnen
to pounce on – sich auf etwas stürzen; shaggy – zottelig

"Ooow!" A **stabbing** pain went through my hand. "The fleece bit me!"

But fleeces can't bite, I thought at the same moment. The fleece wasn't a fleece at all! The fleece was alive. The fleece was a dog! And the dog wasn't lying on Finn! There was no Finn here at all! I turned to the witch.

"You've not got my brother?" I asked in a choky voice.

Jan let his walking stick drop and the woman sighed with relief.

"I'm supposed to have your brother? Children, what on earth is the matter?"

The woman, who introduced herself as Frau Bondje, led us back into the house. Somehow everything looked different now. Had this house seemed so spooky to me? When I looked at it now, I in fact found it really **cosy**. Frau Bondje didn't at all have a big nose either, and her hair wasn't tangled but **curly**. In fact, nothing here was spooky, let alone mad. How embarrassing!

Frau Bondje told us that she was an artist. She made sculptures out of wood and wrote children's books on the side.

Children's books! I thought, ashamed. That's why she collected all those newspaper cuttings about babies and small children. And I'd thought she was a madwoman.

---

to stab – stechen
cosy – gemütlich; curly – kraus

"That's a terrible story," said Frau Bondje, shaking her head, after Jan had told her what had happened.

In the kitchen she fetched some first-aid things from a cupboard and put me on the kitchen table.

"Dog bites are no joke! Does it hurt?"

I couldn't speak any longer. I just sobbed quietly to myself. There was a lump in my throat that I couldn't swallow, however violently I tried.

I didn't even **flinch** when Frau Bondje shook half a litre of **iodine** over the wound. The pain in my heart was so much greater. If Frau Bondje hadn't abducted Finn, then what had happened to him? Where was he?

"We'll ring your parents now," said Frau Bondje and went to the telephone.

I heard my mother's shrill voice.

"Hello?"

She only sounded like that when she was out of her mind with worry. Like when I had jumped out of a second-storey window at primary school to chase my bouncy ball, and had broken my leg. Now she was out of her mind with worry about Finn. And it was my fault because I'd preferred kissing to looking after my little brother.

Frau Bondje pressed the receiver into my hand.

"Mum." My throat produced nothing but croaks. "Mum. I'm so sorry. It's all my fault. I ..."

Mum interrupted me. "Lana. Thank God. Lana. Are you okay? Where are you? Is Jan with you? We've been so worried about you."

---

to flinch – zurückzucken; iodine – Jod

What was she saying? She had been worried about *us*?

"But Finn ..." I wailed.

"Angel. Finn's fine. He hasn't been abducted. Simon told us everything. It was just a misunderstanding. We took Finn with us."

"What?" My feelings **wavered** between incomprehension and relief.

"When we set off, Dad told you that we'd prefer to take Finn with us. You evidently didn't hear him amidst all that kissing."

A cry of delight came from my throat. "My God, Mum, I've never been so relieved in my life as I am now!"

Frau Bondje took the receiver and told my mother how to get to her house. I fell into Jan's arms and we danced around the kitchen like two **drunkards**.

I could already hear the hooting from a long way off.

"They're coming!"

I ran into the yard and flung myself into my parents' arms. Then I dashed over to the car and bent down over the baby seat. There he was. Finn. **As fit as a fiddle**. Unharmed. Happily dribbling. He laughed at me like an innocent angel that didn't know that there were also such things as mad abductors and grave-like torture chambers.

A warm feeling spread through me. And I had to

---

to waver – schwanken
drunkard – Besoffene/r
as fit as a fiddle – quietschfidel

admit that it could well be perfect love. I took Finn out of his seat and held him close to me. He gurgled with pleasure and stroked his tiny hands across my face as if he were trying to say: well, at last, **sisterkins**: it was about time that you said a proper hello to me.

"Yes, you're right," I whispered to him. "It's high time."

My parents said an **effusive** thank you to Frau Bondje.

She laughed. "It doesn't do to joke with your daughter and her boyfriend when they're angry. They're the bravest pair of children I've ever met." Then she turned to us. "You're a great team!"

---

sisterkins – Schwesterchen
effusive – überschwänglich

The real chainsaw murderess

On the way back to our holiday home I was happier than ever in my life before. Dad whistled *Don't worry, be happy*. Mum had put her hand on his upper thigh, and was looking happily at us in the rear-view mirror. And I sat between my best friend and the baby-seat with my sweet little brother. Life could be wonderful.

"We're a great team," laughed Jan.

"We certainly are. The way you threatened her with the stick! *Lana, I'll give you cover!*"

"And the way you fell in the rubbish on the lorry. You've still got a bit of banana skin in your hair." Jan plucked a piece of brown banana skin out of my **fringe** and threw it out of the open window.

Mum turned to us, grinning. "That's what I said: her favourite thing is getting dirty."

I doubled up with laughter. "I'm just wild and stubborn!"

At home, I couldn't keep my hands off Finn at all. I felt as if I'd never properly looked at him yet. Whilst

---

fringe – Pony

Mum and Dad prepared the supper, Jan and I laid Finn down on the fleece. I looked at his feet with their toes that were as small as peanuts. If you rubbed Finn's tummy, he started to chuckle. If you put your index finger in his little hand, he curled his tiny fingers up into a fist which grasped you so hard that you could have carried him round the room by the fingers. His ears were really downy. And he smelled so good. "Like waffle dough," I said to Jan.

"Nah, like **jelly babies**."

"Nah, much better than that. And his eyes are like mine, aren't they?"

Jan inspected us both. "Yes, that's right."

"Of course, he's my brother," I said proudly. "I can't remotely understand now how I could have been so terribly angry with this little creature."

"You were jealous."

I didn't like to hear that, but Jan was, of course, right.

"Yes, I probably was. I should know better at thirteen, shouldn't I?"

Jan grinned.

After supper I helped Mum to bath Finn. It was fantastic fun. Finn seemed to like water just as much as I did. He kicked his little legs around wildly.

"Basketballer's legs," I said.

Mum smiled. "The kidnapping did you good, didn't it?"

I nodded. "Sometimes you only realize what you've got when you think you've lost it."

---

jelly baby – Gummibärchen

"**Crikey**, Lana! I can't cope with so much wisdom from you," laughed Mum, splashing me with water.

I splashed her back. "You're just afraid I'll be wiser than you one day!"

After the bath I put Finn's nappy on him, and proved not to be entirely useless at it. Then I took him to bed and covered him up.

"Sleep tight. I love you lots."

When I went through the living room door, Jan sprang out, armed with an umbrella, and scared me to death.

"Give him back, you witch!" he imitated me.

I switched an imaginary chainsaw on and ran after Jan with a mad killer's face. I chased him through the whole house and finally into the garden. From the garden we ran out into the street.

"I'm the real chainsaw murderess!" I screeched. "I'm going to saw you up into pieces and make a casserole out of you! Dutch Jan Soup with curry and **caraway**!"

As I was just raising my arms to bring down my 'chainsaw', I bumped into an obstacle. I'd run full-pelt into Simon who'd suddenly appeared in the street with Silvie.

"Oops." This situation seemed familiar to me.

Simon looked at me in great **consternation**. Silvie looked at Jan with the same lack of comprehension.

Crikey! – Du meine Güte!
caraway – Kümmel; consternation – Besorgnis

I dropped the invisible chainsaw onto the ground with a silent bump. "Oh, hello. It's you two. I'd forgotten …"

I stopped mid-sentence. I couldn't possibly say out loud that I'd completely forgotten that they existed. After all, Simon was standing in front of me; my boyfriend whom I kissed. But after all the excitement a small **memory-lapse** was surely allowed.

We told Simon and Silvie what had happened.

"It was so insane!" Jan said excitedly. "Lana was so brave."

"Oh, not at all," I replied, embarrassed. "You were the brave one."

"No. You."

"No. You."

"You."

"You."

"Yeah, whatever," Silvie interrupted us, annoyed.

"You really are as hard as nails," said Simon, not very pleased, after we'd told him all the details.

Oh dear. I knew that sentence only too well. Was everything repeating itself now? Crashing into one another. Being as hard as nails. For a moment I was tempted to **atone for** being as hard as nails with a sugary-sweet compliment and to say something like: "I'm sure you'd have been even braver." But only for a moment. Because I then remembered something Jan had said in the worst minutes of the

---

memory-lapse – Gedächtnislücke
to atone for sth – sich für etwas revanchieren

day: *if we manage this, we'll never be afraid of anyone or anything for the rest of our lives.*

Damn! Jan was right. I'd jumped into a moving lorry. I'd **taken on** a chainsaw. I'd risked my life. How could I be afraid of Simon thinking that I was as hard as nails? That was absurd.

"Yes, I'm as hard as nails," I said proudly right into Simon's face.

He was too **gobsmacked** to say anything. Then the four of us sat on the patio and watched the moon slowly rising.

Silvie cuddled up to Jan. "You were so heroic." And in order to emphasize her admiration, she pulled him to her and kissed him long and passionately.

I looked across at Simon. He made no move at all to kiss me. I'd been heroic, too. I'd also earned a bit of admiration. But Simon didn't look proud: he looked somehow offended.

Mum came out onto the patio and brought us something to drink. "Dad and I have decided that we'll have a little party tomorrow. With a barbecue and a bit of music. To celebrate the rescue. And because we're going back home the day after tomorrow."

The day after tomorrow? I hadn't remotely noticed how time was passing. But such a huge amount had happened during these holidays that the hours had raced by like seconds.

---

to take sth on – gegen etwas antreten
gobsmacked – verdattert

"Great idea, Mum!" I cried in delight.

"Simon, let your parents know. And Silvie, you can bring your family, too, if you like. And, of course, we'll invite Frau Bondje, too."

"Great, Mum!"

After I'd drunk up my lemonade, I realized how tired I was. The day had been damned exhausting.

I yawned. "It's late. I'm going to bed."

Simon didn't **stir**. Didn't he even want to say goodnight?

"Goodnight, Simon."

No reaction.

I leant down to him and gave him a kiss on the cheek. "Good night," I said again.

He finally made the effort to reply. "Night."

I was too tired to wonder what was wrong with him. I just wanted to sleep.

Tomorrow was another day. And I'd taken on enough challenges for one day.

---

to stir – sich rühren

So that was it, then

We spent the whole day preparing for the party in the evening. Dad and Jan drove into town to buy **charcoal** while Mum and I shredded the **lettuce** and prepared the dessert. As we did so, we had the radio on loudly and had great fun because Finn squealed almost in time to Sting, Queen and the Backstreet Boys.

"Maybe he'll be a pop star. A professional basketball player and a pop star. Then you'll never stop giving interviews, Mum."

Mum giggled and grabbed a cooking spoon as a microphone. "I hardly ever see my children, you know. But when I'm missing them I just switch the TV on. There's always one of them on some programme or other."

I grabbed the washing-up brush and stood in front of Mum. "And do you believe your parenting had a profound influence on your children's success?"

"Of course. I'm the best mother in the world, you know."

---

charcoal – Holzkohle
lettuce – Kopfsalat

We had to laugh like hysterical hens. The whole day I was cheerful and giggly. I thought about Simon's offended face a couple of times but it didn't spoil my mood.

"Do you want to wear the mini skirt?" Mum asked as we were getting changed for the evening.

I shook my head. "Nah, it's too cold and too impractical."

I put on my favourite jeans and my most comfortable hooded sweatshirt.

Silvie came with her parents, who were very pleased to meet us all.

Silvie introduced Jan. "This is my boyfriend."

Her parents shook Jan's hand, and her father gave him a **matey** thump on the shoulder. "Hello, sports pal."

Crikey, I thought, the next thing is that he'll be asking if Jan can **provide for** his daughter, and then Silvie's mother will be planning the wedding cake.

I preferred to take myself off to Dad at the barbecue.

"Where's Simon got to?" asked Dad.

"Haven't a clue. He'll come."

But first came Frau Bondje. We were delighted to see her. How on earth could I have mistaken this nice woman for a witch and chainsaw murderess?

Frau Bondje gave Jan and me an envelope. "There's a story for you in there."

---

matey – kumpelhaft
to provide for sb – für jmdn. finanziell aufkommen

"You've written a story especially for us?" I asked with disbelief.

Frau Bondje laughed. "Yes, you inspired me."

I wanted to tear the envelope open. "I'll read it aloud at once!"

Frau Bondje stopped me. "You'd be better reading it in a quiet moment when you're back home."

"Okay, if you think so."

Frau Bondje winked at us and nodded.

The Schneiders were the last to arrive. Simon's face was just as reserved as on the previous evening.

"Hi."

"Hi."

He didn't make the slightest attempt to greet me with a kiss. And I had no desire to get a rebuff like yesterday's, so made no attempt either.

We just kept out of one another's way. I grabbed a sausage from the barbecue and bit into it.

"I hope you're not going to **bombard** me again!" cried Mum mock-anxiously in my direction, and went to hide under a garden chair.

I had to laugh. Everyone had to laugh. Only Simon didn't **turn a hair**.

After we'd eaten, Dad put his Barry White CD on and started to dance. He asked Mum and Frau Bondje to dance with him at the same time. Silvie pulled Jan up from his chair and whirled around to the beat. The Schneiders went for it, and Silvie's parents finally joined in, too. Everyone was dancing. Simon

---

to bombard – beschießen
to turn a hair – Gefühle zeigen

and I were the only ones sitting in our chairs like zombies.

Damn it, Lana, I thought to myself, don't let his black mood bring you down. If he doesn't want to dance with you, then just dance on your own. I tried to remember what Silvie had taught me about dancing. How did it go? Shake your head? Circle your hips? Even thinking about the complicated choreography made me feel sick.

I jumped up, **mingled with** the dancers, and simply shut my eyes. Let's see what happens if I switch my brain off, I thought. And then it all happened on its own. My legs moved and called to my arms: join in! My arms didn't need a second invitation, and within a couple of seconds the news had spread across my body. All my available muscles danced. I hadn't the faintest idea what this spectacle looked like from outside. But I didn't care because I was having such great fun. It was so much fun that I completely forgot that Simon looked like a wet weekend. I danced towards him, waved myself around under his nose like an Oriental beauty and tried to get him to stand up.

"Come on. It's fun!"

"Don't want to."

"Why not?"

"Why not? Because. First of all, you spend the whole time not bothering with me, and now I'm supposed to dance with you."

"Who's not bothering with who? Aren't you all

---

to mingle with people – sich unter die Leute mischen

huffy? You didn't even want to say good night yesterday. You ..."

Simon simply went over to the barbecue mid-conversation and heaped sausages onto his plate. That was the last straw.

I stomped over to him, took the plate from his hand, and had to get a grip on myself in order not to chuck every sausage at his head, one by one. "I'd really like to know what I've done to you!"

Simon looked angrily at me and wrenched the plate back out of my hand. "You've been really weird since yesterday," he grumbled.

I grabbed the plate back so violently that half the sausages landed on the ground. "I've been weird?"

As Simon got the plate back under his control, the remaining sausages fell down, too.

"Oh great. **Nice one**!" he yelled at me.

I sighed. What on earth was going on? Why on earth were we quarrelling like this? I had no desire for everyone else to hear our argument.

"Come on, let's go for a little walk. We need to talk," I said, and simply pulled Simon after me.

In the road it was suddenly very quiet. Very faintly you could hear scraps of music and the lively voices.

"Simon, what's ...," I started, but didn't get to finish my sentence.

"Hi."

All of a sudden, Piet and Florian were standing in

---

huffy – verärgert
Nice one! – *ironisch:* Gut gemacht! Volltreffer!

front of us. And all of a sudden, Simon was able to move the corners of his mouth again, and grinned with pleasure.

"Hi."

"We're leaving tomorrow," said Piet.

"Me, too," said Simon. "But we can exchange addresses. Then we could visit each other sometimes."

"Good idea," replied Piet and fished out a piece of paper.

Florian took a pen out of his trouser pocket. Then the three got stuck in and wrote their addresses down.

I watched the scene as if I were watching a play in the theatre. How could Simon exchange addresses with these two defective parking-meters? How could he think they were nice? How could my boyfriend be friends with these idiots? All of a sudden, everything was crystal clear.

"Take care!" Simon waved after Piet and Florian. "They're really nice," he said when the pair were out of sight.

"I don't think so," I said.

Simon immediately pulled a face again.

"Simon, you know what our problem is?"

I had in fact only intended this question to be a way of introducing an explanation, but Simon seemed to have his own ideas about what our problem was.

"There's something wrong with you," he said angrily. "That's the problem. One day you're one thing, and the next day you're something different. I don't at all know what to make of you."

He really was confused. I had to grin. "You know what? You're right. No wonder you haven't got a clue where you stand with me. I really have behaved strangely."

Simon's face lightened. "The way you were yesterday and today was really foul."

"The way I was yesterday and the way I am today is what I'm really like. I'm just like I was when you met me. A pretty wild child." I giggled. But Simon didn't seem to find it funny. "We don't go together," I added, and had to stop myself from cackling loudly. "We go together like the Hobbits and the Orcs. Like Heino and Britney Spears. Like ..." I could think of loads of comparisons, and I'd have become more and more worked up if Simon had let me.

"Listen," he interrupted me. "I'm finishing with you."

I was gobsmacked. *I* was just in the process of finishing with *him!* But I was just making the biggest effort to explain to him in flowery colours why we didn't go together. His **sledgehammer** method left me speechless for a moment.

"Exactly," I then said. "We're finished."

So that was it, I thought. It happens that quickly. I quickly checked my inner self and examined whether it twitched or burned anywhere. But nothing hurt. My heart was beating calmly. My stomach was going about its normal business. My throat was a bit tight. I felt perfectly fine.

"Great. Well, then ..." I said, relieved.

---

sledgehammer – Vorschlaghammer

I'd wanted to say that we could carry on with the party in peace now that we'd sorted everything out. But Simon wasn't listening to me any longer. He turned and went straight back into the garden. I had trouble catching him up.

I enjoyed the rest of the party to the full. Now that we weren't together, Simon's turned-down mouth no longer bothered me. Turned-down mouths of ex-boyfriends who had themselves finished the relationship really were not my problem.

I chatted for a long time to Frau Bondje, and told her in glorious technicolour what kinds of terrible fantasies I'd had about her. She laughed her head off.

When she left, we both promised to write to one another.

"You tell me what you've been doing, and I'll write stories about it," she said happily.

"Deal."

Shortly afterwards Herr Schneider said they were leaving. I'd not spoken to Simon again during the rest of the party. He hadn't responded to my attempts to give him encouraging smiles. He obviously thought that finishing with someone meant you had to ignore them.

Now we were standing opposite one another in the doorway. How absurd if we don't even say goodbye, I thought. After all, we've kissed each other pretty often and pretty intimately. We can't suddenly act as if we were two strangers.

"Well, then," I said in a friendly manner. "Have a good journey home."

Simon looked at his feet. "Hmm. You, too," he growled.

I was desperate to say something nice. Somehow or another I wanted to find a nice way of ending things.

"You're a really good kisser," I said.

Simon raised his head and gave a crooked grin. Bingo, I thought. Compliments have pulled him again.

"You, too," he said, then turned and disappeared.

So that's it then, I thought. I shrugged my shoulders and went to bed.

I don't believe it!

It was difficult to get up the next morning. Whilst Mum and Dad were loading up the car, Jan and I grabbed our swimming things for one last time and ran to the beach.

"Ritual beach-farewell!" I squealed.

"You don't mind if I make it my ritual, too, do you?" Jan yelled back.

"Not in the slightest! If anyone can **nick** my rituals, it's you!"

We knelt before the sea in the sand and threw our arms in the air like two Muslim worshippers. Then we bent our heads and upper bodies.

"Sea, thank you for existing!"

"Please don't dry out before we come the next time."

"Stay as salty as you are."

"And wet."

We laughed our heads off and slipped out of our shorts.

"Is Simon coming over again to say goodbye?" Jan wanted to know.

---

to nick – klauen

So far I'd told neither him nor Mum and Dad what had happened between Simon and me yesterday evening. They had been surprised to see that Simon and I had avoided one another the whole evening, but had been satisfied with my explanation. "Simon feels sick," I'd said. "Too many sausages."

I just hadn't felt like exposing myself to all the questions: so aren't you at all sad? You were so mad about him, and now you're acting as if everything was fine?

How was I supposed to explain that the thing between Simon and me had been more or less a … **slip**? A kind of mistake.

I looked at Jan and shook my head. "Nah. He's not coming."

"Is he coming to the house?"

I shook my head again. "He's not coming at all."

"Why not?"

I sighed. There was no point in keeping it to myself any longer. I'd have to say something sooner or later. "We split up yesterday."

Jan was silent for a moment, then frowned, then shrugged his shoulders. "Was the whole thing a kind of mistake?"

I nodded, flabbergasted. How did he know?

"You know, I think I actually like a different kind of boy," I said.

"So what kind of boy do you like?"

I took a deep breath. Well. What kind of boys *did*

---

slip – Ausrutscher

I like? I hadn't thought about it that deeply. I now knew what kind I *didn't* like. That was, boys who were always telling boring stories; boys for whom girls had to act like **trained** King Poodles. The kind that didn't have a sense of humour and couldn't even be a bit mad every now and then.

"Hmm. I think I like boys I can have adventures with, who I can roll around laughing with. Boys who enjoy getting into **scrapes** as much as I do. Just boys who aren't so exhausting and aren't boring. Boys with imagination. But you find me one." I looked at Jan and shrugged my shoulders.

"Cooo-eee, I'm he-e-e-e-re!"

Silvie came running across the beach, waving **with all her might**. She flew into Jan's arms, making a dreadful noise.

All of a sudden, I felt terribly **superfluous**. That was undoubtedly because up until then we'd been on a couples holiday, and now I wasn't part of a couple any more.

I simply turned away. After all, I was here to say goodbye to the sea. And a proper farewell involved a swim.

I plunged into the waves and let the cool water refresh me one last time. Enjoy! Farewell! Enjoy! Farewell! I thought forcedly. But I couldn't remotely think of enjoying it. My heart was thudding like mad in my chest.

---

trained – *hier:* dressiert; scrape – Patsche, Klemme
with all one's might – mit aller Kraft
superfluous – überflüssig

Was my **circulation** collapsing? Was the water too cold? And what was wrong with my neck? Why on earth did it keep turning of its own accord to the shore? And my eyes? Why couldn't they stop looking over at Jan and Silvie?

I think I like boys I can have adventures with, who I can roll around laughing with. Boys who enjoy getting into scrapes as much as I do. Just boys who aren't so exhausting and aren't boring. Boys with imagination. But you find me one.

Oh my God. O-o-oh my G-o-o-o-od! I don't believe it!!! It could only be a heart defect! It was absolute madness!

I looked, **spellbound**, at the beach, where Silvie and Jan were kissing. What was that? I rubbed my eyes. Was I hallucinating? Instead of Silvie I could see another girl in Jan's arms. Oh God! This other girl was me!

I quickly dived underwater. Could you wash out hallucinations? Perhaps it helped if you cooled your head down? Perhaps I should just hold my breath for a bit. I absolutely had to get a grip on myself.

I stayed underwater and listened to the silence. Everything's fine, I told myself. When you come up, everything will be as it was before.

Something suddenly tugged at my hair. And before I knew what was going on, I'd been torn from the still underwater world and up to the surface.

"Lana! Are you mad?" Jan's face was completely shocked. "I thought you'd drowned."

---

circulation – Kreislauf; spellbound – gebannt, fasziniert

I was much too flabbergasted to reply. Jan was still holding me tightly in his arms. And I felt his hand as clearly as if it were red-hot.

"Everything's fine," I said quickly, set off, and swam back to the shore.

I gathered my things together and raced off in the direction of the dunes. Nothing was fine. Oh, why had he pulled me out of the water? I should have stayed under for longer, then everything would surely have been alright again.

I kicked the beach pavilion so hard that it hurt horribly. But I didn't care. I kept kicking it. No! No! No! I kept thinking. It could only be a stupid mistake.

"Stop that at once! That's **wilful damage** to property!" The ice-cream seller made an angry leap in my direction.

"Is it possible that you can't find something just because it's right in front of your nose?" I asked him, my eyebrows raised in desperation.

The ice-cream seller looked at me, confused. He opened and shut his mouth repeatedly without answering.

---

wilful damage – vorsätzliche Beschädigung

Battle of the killer hormones

I stomped up the dunes. Everything was clattering around in my head. These stupid rituals were to blame for everything. When I'd said hello to the sea, I'd fallen in love with Simon, and when I said goodbye today, I'd … No, I hadn't! No! No! No! But why hadn't I fallen in love all the other years when I was going through my rituals?

It slowly **dawned on** me. It was the hormones that were to blame for everything. Hormones were damned dangerous. Ever since these hormones had captured my body, I had made one mistake after the other. I'd barely uncovered one mistake when the next one happened.

But this time I'd put a stop to these hormones! I'd ban myself from falling in love. Oh yes, I'd need strong measures. These hormones were **unpredictable**. I had to protect myself against them. I'd stop them!

When I got back, Dad was just loading the car. He had put a cassette of his favourite German rock

---

to dawn on sb – jmdm. dämmern
unpredictable – unvorhersagbar, unberechenbar

singer into the car stereo and was singing along at the top of his voice whilst he desperately tried to stuff all the suitcases and bags and carrier bags with mussels into the overflowing car.

"Tausend Mal berührt. Tausend Mal ist nichts passiert. Tausendundeine Nacht und es hat zoom gemacht ..."

Had my hormones now joined forces with Dad's old cassette?

"Your Klaus Lage is completely stupid, Dad," I grumbled. "How can you listen to that rubbish?"

Dad's jaw dropped. "I like it," he said, shrugging his shoulders.

I **rewound** the song. With every line I became more angry. "As if you'd suddenly fall in love after such a long time. With your best friend. It's totally stupid."

As I was rewinding it for a second time, Jan and Silvie came strolling up to us.

"Well, you two. Is it hard to say goodbye?" asked Dad.

"Oh yes," answered Silvie with a sigh.

"Of course," said Jan.

Mum came to the car with Finn in her arms. "Everything's ready. We can set off."

"So, Lana. Bye, then." Silvie held out her hand and I had to shake it for better or for worse.

"Bye," I said dryly.

Apart from the fact that you use tampons, I think everything about you is pretty stupid, I thought. I bit my tongue so that I didn't say it out loud.

---

to rewind – zurückspulen

"We're bound to see each other a fair bit when I visit Jan," she piped.

I had to hold on to my hand, or else it would surely have given her a whack on the chin.

I stole a glance out of the back window. Silvie was just getting ready for a farewell kiss. I dug my fingernails into the car seat. I couldn't watch!

Of course, nobody asked me, but if anyone *had* asked me, I'd have said: Jan and Silvie can only be a mistake.

The car journey seemed terribly long. I spent the whole time trying to act as relaxed as possible whilst the battle of the giants was going on inside me. The army of the killer hormones on the Mistake Campaign against **sole warrior** Lana.

And then Mum wanted to get me into a conversation.

"Are you sad about Simon?"

"Yes, I am!" I said.

It wasn't a bad thing if she thought the pain of parting had left its mark on me. It was better than her being able to read me like an open book. An open, rather stupid book with the absurd title: *I'm in love with my best friend.* Subtitle: *I'm completely nuts.*

Mum's **clairvoyant** skills didn't seem to be on top form today. Thank God!

"You can write and visit each other," she said.

"Mum, I don't want to talk about it."

---

sole warrior – Alleinkämpfer/in, -krieger/in
clairvoyant – hellseherisch

"That's fine, sweetheart."

At that moment Jan turned to me and grinned.

Oh heavens all those years I'd never seen that Jan had lips in his face. Well, I probably had seen them, but I'd somehow taken them to be unimportant frames for his mouth, frames that moved when he was talking, eating and laughing. It had never occurred to me that they looked terribly soft and seductive. And it would have seemed completely mad to me if I'd thought they'd arouse the need in me to stroke them gently with my little finger.

I realized that my little finger was trying to move in the direction of Jan's lips, grabbed it with my other hand **without further ado**, and held onto it tightly.

"Shall we play basketball tomorrow?" Jan's lips wanted to know.

Did he absolutely have to ask me something now when I needed all my concentration to keep my finger in check? Couldn't he wait until next week when I'd have these stupid hormones under control again? When everything was as it used to be?

"Earth to Lana. What about it?" Jan asked impatiently.

"I don't know yet," I croaked back, quickly turning away and staring out of the window.

But after a few seconds my head shot back round in Jan's direction. Why had these fine blond hairs suddenly appeared on the brown skin of his neck? And why did the leather ribbon round his neck look

---

without further ado – kurzerhand

so damned good with the little blond hairs and the brown skin?

In one go, I sat on my hands. That way I could control all my fingers at the same time.

I forbade myself to look at Jan's neck for the whole of the rest of the journey. In fact, I didn't look forwards at all, just sideways out of the window until we had finally got through a horrendous five-hour traffic jam near Aachen.

Dad stopped the car outside Jan's house. My hands had completely gone to sleep under my bum, and now had terrible pins and needles. I had to shake them wildly to bring them back to life.

"That was a great holiday," Jan said to Mum and Dad. "Thanks a million again for letting me come with you!"

If only he'd gone to stay with his grandma and her ornamental cushions, I thought **involuntarily**. Then I wouldn't be in this stupid dilemma now. This holiday just threw everything into chaos.

"Bye, Lana. I'll ring you tomorrow, okay?"

"Hmm." I couldn't get a word out.

But Jan didn't let it irritate him. Without any warning, he grabbed hold of me unasked, and pressed me close to him.

I rummaged around in Dad's cassettes and found the Klaus Lage song.

"I don't want to be disturbed!" I called into the kitchen.

---

involuntary – unfreiwillig

I locked my bedroom door. Alone at last. Finally in my familiar four walls. Finally nobody around me from whom I had to hide my hormonal chaos.

I knelt on the floor, put the cassette in and put the headphones on.

"Tausend Mal berührt. Tausend Mal ist nichts passiert."

This Klaus Lage song really is **beyond good and evil**! I thought, repeatedly rewinding it so that I could write down the words.

After an hour and a half I knew the song off by heart, and my tummy was rumbling.

I went into the kitchen where Mum was just flicking through the TV guide.

"*My Best Friend's Wedding* is on tonight," she said.

"Load of rubbish," I snapped.

"Why?" Mum wanted to know.

"Well, I ask you. Julia Roberts has been friends with this guy for years and doesn't notice anything. And when this guy wants to marry someone else, she notices, all of a sudden, that it doesn't suit her. It's nonsense."

Mum grinned. "I think it's romantic."

Blimey, I thought. Maybe there was a defective gene in our family. Dad listened to Klaus Lage, Mum liked *My Best Friend's Wedding*, and I . . .!

"Things like that never happen in real life!" I said.

Dad came into the kitchen. He had evidently heard our conversation from in the hall.

---

beyond good and evil – jenseits von Gut und Böse
Blimey! – Zum Kuckuck!

"Oh yes, they do," he said. "It happens all the time. My colleague Frau Helmer, for example. She spent years crying on the shoulder of her best friend from the **sandpit** because she was always falling for the wrong men. And what do you think happened? One day he found a rather different way of comforting her. You know what I mean. And now they want to get married."

"Yes. That happens a lot," Mum agreed. "Aunt Ludo and Uncle Bert, for example. Best friends. Frau Sommer from the flower shop and her husband. Best friends for years. Hans Zimmer and ..."

I stopped listening. Was it possible? Could it be that my hormones weren't acting crazy? I pondered. Would a record company release a song if it were complete nonsense? Hardly. Would Hollywood make a film with Julia Roberts if it made no sense at all? Hardly. Aunt Ludo and Uncle Bert were pretty okay. They surely wouldn't do anything completely crazy. Hardly.

All of a sudden, I felt much better. Mum and Dad were still busily exchanging news about couples who'd been best friends beforehand. I strolled into Finn's room. He was lying **contentedly** in his **cot**, and looked at me expectantly.

"Dear brother," I whispered, and leant over him. "What on earth should I do?" Finn made a squealing noise.

---

sandpit – Sandkasten
contented – zufrieden
cot – Kinderbett

"You think I should stop agonizing?"

Finn raised his little arms and did something rather like shadow-boxing.

"You think I should fight?"

Finn hit himself on the nose with a little hand.

"You think I should blow Silvie out of the water? Competition keeps the market alive, doesn't it?"

Finn kicked his legs like mad.

"You think I shouldn't wait another second, but should go for it?"

Finn crowed like a hen gone mad.

"That was a command? Okay. **I'm out of here**."

I pressed a big kiss onto Finn's cheek. "You know what? It's great having a brother you can ask for advice. I'll repay you when you're going through puberty."

I'm out of here. – Ich gehe schon.

Crash! Bang! Zoom!

"Is Jan in?"

Jan's mother shook her head. "He's out on his bike. He was going to see you."

"Strange. Then we should in fact have bumped into one another."

Jan's mother shrugged her shoulders. "There was something he wanted to do beforehand."

"Thanks. See you soon. Bye."

I threw myself at the pedals and cycled back home. I was just cycling over the crossroads on the main street when I saw a red mountain bike turning the corner.

"Jan!"

He didn't hear me. I cycled like mad in order to catch up with him. He had something in his hand. And as I got nearer, I saw that it was a bunch of flowers.

"Jan!"

Why couldn't he hear me? I sped up and managed to get quite close to him. Now I could also see why he couldn't hear me. He had earplugs in his ears and his discman in his trouser pocket.

I got onto a level with him and reached my arm

out in order to tap him on the shoulder. Big mistake! Our bikes became entangled for a fraction of a second.

We both lost control. As if in slow motion, I saw the catastrophe heading for us. Jan was shocked to death. For him, of course, the whole thing came from nowhere. His eyes wide open, he turned to me before losing his balance and flying off the bike, his arms **flailing** wildly.

At the same moment I felt as if the ground were being torn from under my feet. My bike briefly crashed into the kerb, and I made a high curve as I sailed through the air.

That's it, Lana, shot through my head. Now you won't be able to tell him that everything went zoom because everything will go bang instead. I was still marvelling at how much and how clearly you could think whilst you were flying through the air when I had a surprisingly soft landing.

Was that a cloud already? But when I turned my head, I saw that I'd landed on Jan.

"O-o-o-w!" he moaned under my weight.

I quickly checked to see whether all my arms and legs did as they were told, established that everything functioned perfectly, and rolled quickly off Jan.

"Jan, are you okay?"

"You weigh at least three tonnes," he moaned.

"Does it hurt?"

Jan felt his stomach all over. "Not too much. Just a crushed **liver**, a torn **intestine** and a broken

---

to flail – fuchteln; liver – Leber; intestine – Darm

heart," he said deadly seriously. "What about you? Are you okay?"

"Yes, yes. Just a double **pelvic fracture**, an open fracture to my leg, and violent amnesia."

We both suppressed a giggle, rolled over towards one another, and looked at each other in mock-confusion.

"I think I've got amnesia, too. Who am I? Who are you?" blathered Jan.

At that moment a car stopped with a screech of brakes. A young woman jumped out of the car and ran towards us.

"Oh my God! Are you okay?"

"We've got amnesia," I said earnestly.

"Pardon?"

"Memory loss," Jan explained patiently. "Haven't you ever seen *Emergency Room*?"

He stood up and helped me back onto my feet. Only then did we see what was what. Our bikes were lying in the gutter, pretty much demolished. We had landed in a front garden, right on top of a heap of freshly mown grass.

The woman looked us up and down. "Do you need an ambulance?"

Jan shook his head. "Everything's fine."

"Do you want me to drive you somewhere?"

I shook my head. "We have to remember where we live first."

For a moment the woman wasn't sure whether we might not have severe concussion after all.

---

pelvic fracture – Beckenbruch

"It was just a joke," Jan said quickly.

Shaking her head, the woman got back into her car and drove off.

"Joke? Not on your life," I said. "Or do you perhaps know who I am?"

Jan looked at me with concentration. "No, I've never seen you before. Do you know anything about me?"

"Nah. Not a clue." I plucked the grass from Jan's hair.

"Oh, well," said Jan thoughtfully. "Heaven only knows whether we had anything to do with one another in the past."

"Yes, but you know what? Collisions are always fate. I *do* remember that."

"Hmm. It seems that we've got no choice but to find out bit by bit who we are."

"Yes. I think I'm a girl. That much is clear."

We had to laugh. Jan and I picked our bikes up. In the middle of the road lay a sad heap of greenery. Squashed flat.

Jan scraped it off the ground. "That was once a bunch of flowers. For you. It's dead now."

"What had I done to deserve flowers?"

"If only I could remember." Jan scratched his head.

"In fact, losing your memory wouldn't be bad at all," I said thoughtfully.

Jan looked at me questioningly.

"Well," I **hummed and hawed**. "Then you might forget Silvie."

---

to hum and haw – in der Rede stocken

Jan looked at me as if I'd been speaking Chinese. "Silvie? Silvie? With the best will in the world, I don't remember a Silvie."

"If only." I didn't at all feel like joking any more. "Then you might not remember either that I'm your best mate."

Jan looked at me wide eyed. "What do you mean?"

I took a deep breath, remembered Finn's emphatic crowing, and decided not to hesitate any longer. "I mean I don't want to be your best friend any more."

"What? Why not?"

Jesus, this really wasn't easy. Jan didn't get what I was trying to say.

"No. Not that. I *do* still want to be your best friend. But just differently."

Jan shrugged his shoulders. Why was it so complicated?

"Earth to Jan. Are you really so slow on the uptake? I don't want to be *just* your best friend any more. I want ... I want ... I want to be the one you write poems for."

So, now I'd said it. Now the earth could open up and swallow me.

"I feel so stupid," I stammered. "It's just that this Klaus Lage said that it could still go zoom if it hadn't gone zoom thousands of times already. And then I thought ... But Klaus Lage is probably an idiot. And Julia Roberts, too. And Aunt Ludo. And anyway, I'm sure it's just the hormones. And ..."

I got no further with my **disjointed** stammering.

---

disjointed – ohne Zusammenhang

Jan had pulled a piece of paper out of his trouser pocket, and handed it over to me. "The poem wasn't for Silvie. She's never seen it," he said. "And it wasn't finished then either. Now it's finished."

I looked enquiringly at him.

"Read it," he said. I read.

Your hair is as soft as wool,
I like you like mad.
Your eyes shine like the stars.
I like you so much.
When you play basketball like a star
I find you simply wonderful.
All girls should be like you.
But I'd like to have you all to myself.
How on earth can I tell you?
I can't just ask you.
You'd be sure to laugh.
I don't want to make a fool of myself.
I'm sure you just want to stay my best friend.
And yet I still have to write this to you.

"I was just on the way to see you, to give it to you." Jan looked at the tips of his shoes.

I was speechless. "You ... you ... the whole time I ..." I blathered. "And Silvie?"

"That was just because you and Simon ..."

"A mistake?"

Jan nodded.

We stood by our smashed-up bikes for a minute that seemed as long as the whole history of the universe, and said nothing.

I could barely think either. The whole situation was just too ... too ... too ... strange. I started to chuckle involuntarily. Jan looked up from his shoes and looked enquiringly at me. Then he chuckled, too. And before we knew it, we were killing ourselves laughing.

"God, that's gross!" I **spluttered**.

"Completely mad!" yelled Jan.

"You and me!"

"It's so mad!"

"Completely insane!"

"Gaga!"

"Weird!"

"Wicked!"

We held our stomachs.

"Ow! I can't go on!"

"It's too much!"

We fell back, screeching, onto the heap of grass. It took us at least five minutes to calm down. Barely had one of us regained control over their **diaphragm** than the other started to laugh again. It was terribly **contagious**.

"I can't go on," I moaned. "Stop!"

When we finally managed to remain serious, we rolled towards one another.

"So what do we do now?" asked Jan.

"I don't know. What do you do in a situation like this?"

We grinned. We knew very well what to do in a

---

to splutter – stottern; diaphragm – Zwerchfell
contagious – ansteckend

situation like this. And thanks to Silvie and Simon, we also knew how to do it. But for God's sake, kissing your best friend was completely different.

"It's too strange." Jan took the words out of my mouth.

"We don't have to rush things," I said.

Jan nodded. "We have all the time in the world."

"Exactly. We've known one another for so long. A couple of days more or less won't matter."

We stood up, grabbed our bikes, which were ready for the scrap-heap, and strolled along the road. Everything felt so unreal. Although I must have strolled down the road with Jan a thousand times before, it felt quite unfamiliar.

We pushed our bikes with one hand, and with the other hand we touched each other as if by chance with every step. And every one of these touches was like a little electric shock. We kept looking at one another at the same moment, held the other's gaze for a couple of seconds, and then turned our heads away, embarrassed.

When we'd walked half way in silence with our arms constantly touching one another by chance, we both reached for the other's hand and held it tightly.

We're holding hands, I thought in astonishment. And my hand felt damned good.

When we got home, we put our bikes in the garage.

"Hello, you two!"

Mum and Dad were just coming out of the door with Finn in the buggy.

"We're going for a walk. Are you coming?" asked Mum.

"No-o."

"No-o."

Mum looked at me with her **x-ray** vision. Then a grin spread across her face. "Well, we don't want to disturb you any further," she said, and energetically pulled Dad away.

"What's the matter?" Dad asked unsuspectingly.

"I was right," I could hear Mum saying. "Do you remember the first day of the holidays ...?"

When they were **out of earshot,** Jan looked at me, embarrassed.

"She's clairvoyant when it comes to these things," I said, shrugging my shoulders.

Jan grinned. "And it's no secret any more either."

When we were in my room, I put the Klaus Lage cassette on.

"Listen."

We lay on the floor and listened to the song a couple of times.

"Now we've already got a song," said Jan.

"Yes. Our own song," I sighed. Then I sat up abruptly and beamed. "And we've already got a story of our own!"

Jan got it immediately. "Yes, Frau Bondje's story!"

I dug the envelope out of my suitcase, which I hadn't yet unpacked, and began to read. *"Lana, Jan and the Chainsaw Murderess."*

---

x-ray – Röntgenstrahl; out of earshot – außer Hörweite

We had to grin. And we had to keep stopping mid-story because we couldn't stop laughing.

Frau Bondje had turned our rescue mission into a hysterically funny story about a **cunning** detective team. In her story Jan and Lana, brave and mad, did actually rescue a baby from the claws of an evil woman.

"Jan and Lana," I read, *"waved to the nice family once again and then turned towards the sea. 'Enough rescuing for today', said Lana. They stomped up the dunes. The sun was just setting, a spectacular red. 'We're a damn good team,' said Jan. Then he turned to Lana and took her hand. 'We're the best team,' said Lana. And as the sun sank into the sea with a silent plop, their two heads moved closer and closer together. End."*

We were both flabbergasted.

"Are all women clairvoyants?" asked Jan.

"If what I'm thinking right now actually happens in the next few minutes, then yes," I said quietly.

Jan grinned.

And as Frau Bondje's story floated down to the ground with a silent plop, our heads moved closer and closer together.

---

cunning – schlau, listig